# Hooray for children's church

## Lisa Flinn & Barbara Younger

Abingdon Press

HOORAY FOR CHILDREN'S CHURCH

Lisa Flinn and Barbara Younger

*Copyright © 1995 by Abingdon Press*

**Library of Congress Cataloging-in-Publication Data**

Flinn, Lisa, 1951–
    Hooray for children's church / Lisa Flinn & Barbara Younger.
      p.    cm.
    ISBN 0-687-00577-9 (spiral bound : alk. paper)
    1. Worship (Religious education)   I. Younger, Barbara, 1954–
II.  Title.
    BV1522.F57    1995
    264′.0083′3—dc20                    95-18226
                                                    CIP

00 01 02 03 04—10 9 8 7 6

MANUFACTURED IN THE UNITED STATES OF AMERICA

*To Jane McIver,*
teacher extraordinaire,
and in memory of Mr. Strudwick
and
all of the good times in Strudwick Hall

# Contents

# INTRODUCTION

*Looking for wonderful, complete programs for your Children's Church? Then you're looking for a book that offers creative storytelling with a clear biblical message. You'll need fun games, crafts, prayers, and songs that explore and apply the message. And you want music that affirms and strengthens the spirit in your children.* Hooray for Children's Church *is just what you're looking for.*

*The four- to six-year-olds in your congregation will delight in these Children's Church programs that are designed just for their imaginations, attention spans, energy level, and abilities. Your Children's Church will be a happy place for young churchgoers, and their parents will appreciate the time their children spend exploring the Bible and the Christian faith.*

Hooray for Children's Church *offers you fifty-two weeks of spirit-filled programs that will work in any time period from thirty to sixty minutes. Leaders, whether new recruits or experienced volunteers, will appreciate the easy to follow format, the reproducible activity pages, and the helpful suggestions for organizing and running a Children's Church. Care has been taken to limit craft and music supplies to those listed in the front of the book. Create your own Children's Church Kit with simple props that are used in many of the book's activities.*

*No doubt about it, this is the book you're looking for. Here's to happy children, happy leaders, and a happy church. Hooray!*

# How to Use This Book

*Hooray for Children's Church* is organized into nine sections. Each section focuses on a theme that will help young children explore the Bible and the Christian faith. The programs may be used in any order. You may choose a program from one section one week and another section the next week, or you may move through the book section by section. When you have used a program, initial and date it, along with making any notes as to how you might adjust the program another time. You'll find a section just for holidays. You may want to use each holiday program at the appropriate time in the church year. There are other programs in the book that work as holiday programs too: "Mary" (Advent or Christmas); "Jesus Is Born" (Advent or Christmas); "Parents Protect Us" (Epiphany); and "God's Son" (Easter).

The length of Children's Church will vary from church to church. The book's programs are designed to accommodate a thirty- to sixty-minute time period. Music and Movement, Sharing, Listening, Praying, and Exploring will take around thirty to forty minutes. Snacking and More Exploring will add about twenty more minutes to the program.

To staff Children's Church you will need one person to lead the program. If program leaders will alternate from week to week, you may want each leader to have a copy of this book, or have several copies that can be passed around from leader to leader. When working with young children, it's always best to have a helper, especially in the event of an emergency. You should definitely plan on a helper for every additional group of ten to twelve children. Many teenagers enjoy working with young children and will be glad to offer their services.

The programs are designed for children ages four to six. While some of the activities may be a bit challenging for three-year-olds, if your church chooses to include them, children this age will be glad to join in the fun. If you have children a year or two older than six, the themes and activities will appeal to them, too.

*Hooray for Children's Church* is written to be easy to use and fun for children and leaders. Look over the program early in the week. You'll be amazed how relaxed you feel on Saturday night!

Each program follows the same format:

## BIBLE VERSE

A line of scripture (NRSV) appears at the beginning of each program. The verse forms the basis for the program's message, story, and activities.

## MESSAGE

This is a simple statement of the biblical point of the program.

## OPENING

After greeting the children and getting them settled, begin Children's Church with Music and Movement. The section that follows, "Opening with Music and Movement," addresses using music with young children and suggests simple music and movement games. Recommended time for Music and Movement is about ten minutes, but if you need a program that runs only thirty minutes, you may want to shorten the Opening. Music and Movement activities can also be added at the end of Children's Church to expand a program that has run shorter than you anticipated.

**Listening, Sharing, and Praying** are included each week, but their order within the program varies.

## LISTENING

This section features either a passage read directly from the Bible, a paraphrase of a Bible passage, or a story or situation that illustrates the biblical message. Creative storytelling techniques are used to capture the children's attention and help them listen to what is being said. When reading and talking to young children, eye contact does wonders in keeping their attention. Maintain a calm yet enthusiastic voice and speak slowly but clearly. Since some of the stories are more complicated than others, it's best to practice reading or telling them beforehand.

## PRAYING

The prayers are written to help young children understand that when they pray, they are talking to God. A variety of age appropriate prayers and prayer techniques are included.

## SHARING

This is a time to give children a turn to talk and to express their thoughts. It's best to begin at one place in the circle and move around the circle from child to child. Children should listen carefully when others are talking and not interrupt anyone. Children who do not want to talk should not be forced to say something. On the other hand, those who have a lot to say can be encouraged to just make one comment during Sharing.

## EXPLORING

This section includes a variety of creative activities to help children explore the program's message: drama, crafts, reproducible activity pages, children's modeling dough fun, songs, and games. Some of the activities take more preparation than others. Supplies needed are limited to the items in the Children's Church Kit, and the craft and music lists at the end of this section.

You will notice a difference in skill levels among your children. Craft activities, coloring in particular, can take a short amount of time for some children and others will seem to work forever. Keep plain white paper and crayons handy to give to children who finish before the others.

## SNACKING

If a snack is to be served at your Children's Church, consider the snack suggestions included with each program. If you want a simpler snack, keep cookies and juice on hand.

## MORE EXPLORING

These activities are designed to extend Children's Church up to sixty minutes. Most take less preparation than the activities in Exploring.

## TEACHING TIPS

If you are new at working with young children, take heart. All experienced teachers were beginners, too. Soon enough you will develop your own teaching style and rapport with the children. Here are just a few tips:

Learn the names of your children as soon as possible. Sharing time is a good time to have children say their names. Consider name tags if your group is large.

Be sensitive to the needs of children with handicapping conditions. Assign a helper to any child who needs a great deal of assistance. Keep in mind, too, that home situations, personalities, and skill and interest levels will differ from child to child.

Talk with parents. They know their children best and may be able to give you helpful tips in working with their child. Don't hesitate to discuss problems and concerns with parents. Remember, too, that parents love nothing better than to hear happy comments or anecdotes about their children.

Try not to allow disturbances to stop the momentum of the program. Appoint a safekeeping place for trinkets such as toy trucks, dolls, or loose hair ribbons to rest until Children's Church is finished, as children may play with these items instead of listening to the program. Make sure children are comfortable, especially when asked to sit and listen. A circle works well as everyone has his or her own space. Consider separating two children who are being disruptive. Whenever possible, let helpers deal with children who are unhappy or causing problems.

Your goal is to make Children's Church a happy, secure place where children can learn and grow as Christians.

## EQUIPMENT AND SUPPLIES

The space you use for Children's Church need not be large, but there should be enough room for the children to move about during games. You'll need a table and chairs for crafts, and chairs or a rug for circle time.

Reproducible activity pages are included for each section. It's a good idea to go ahead and photocopy all of these at one time to save Sunday morning rushes to the photocopier.

The Children's Church Kit consists of items that are creatively used in the programs. Gather these items and store them at church, perhaps in an attractive carton or drawstring laundry bag.

**For the Children's Church Kit you'll need:**
a bed sheet (solid color, top sheet)
a baby doll
a baby blanket
a ball (eight to twelve inches wide)
a rock (four to six inches wide)
a handbell
a basket (generous size)
a container of pennies (two pennies per child)
modeling dough, wax paper, and plastic knives

**Craft supplies you'll need:**
brad fasteners (use caution with children under
    four years of age)
crayons
8½-by-11-inch white paper
shelf or craft paper on a roll (at least 100 feet)
9-by-12-inch construction paper in assorted colors
    (extra green and brown)
glue
paper plates (9 inch diameter, plain white with
    fluted edge)
old magazines with colorful photographs
    (women's magazines, parenting, nature)
hole punch

luncheon size paper bags
4-by-6-inch plain white index cards
stapler
safety scissors (for each child)
cellophane tape
masking tape (for mounting artwork on walls)
foil stars
yarn

**Music Supplies you'll need:**
a tape recorder
a songbook and tape of Bible songs
rhythm instruments (optional)

# Opening with Music and Movement

Each week, open Children's Church with Music and Movement activities. Young children love to sing, listen to music, and move about with lively games. Depending on the length of your Children's Church, you can decide just how long you would like the opening to last; ten minutes seems about right.

## MUSIC

There are several excellent Christian songbooks with accompanying cassette tapes that feature songs written especially for young children. Simple hand motions are included with many of the songs. Each session in this book suggests four songs from *Sing a New Song: Songs and Activities for Young Children* (Abingdon Press, 1993). The songs are also available on a split-track cassette tape. To play the tape you'll need a tape recorder that works well and has plenty of volume. If your tape recorder depends on batteries, make certain you keep an extra supply on hand. Not only will you want to play the cassette tape during the opening, but you will find other times, such as during a game or art activity, when the tape can be played.

Every week, sing two or three songs with your group. As your children become familiar with the songs, you will want to sing one or two they know and then introduce a new one. Consider selecting a child each week to be the "Children's Church Choir Director." The director gets to pick his or her favorite song for the group to sing. Many of the songs on the tape can be coordinated with the Children's Church theme for the week, although this isn't necessary. As you sing with the children, don't feel timid if your voice isn't ready for the choir. Children want to hear your voice and see your enthusiasm; they aren't concerned if you sing off-key.

Along with music from the tape, you may want to introduce your children to some of the simpler hymns from your hymnal. Children like to hear songs sung in the "big church." If your church uses a liturgy or choral responses, teach children some of this music. In churches where children come straight to Children's Church without going to the big church first, consider taking them into the church on occasion to hear the music. If your children are enthusiastic singers, you may want to have them sing some of the songs they've learned for the congregation. Adults and older kids in the congregation love to hear and see the little ones perform.

A guest musician is always welcome in Children's Church. Ask someone to come and accompany the children on the piano one Sunday. You may have church members who play other instruments who would enjoy playing for Children's Church. Don't overlook older children who are learning to play an instrument. Let children see that there are many ways to praise God with music, from the piano to the clarinet to the kazoo!

Rhythm instruments can be lots of fun and will often draw reluctant singers into the spirit of the music. Most toy, educational, and church supply catalogs offer rhythm instruments. If you don't want to purchase them, make your own. Here are a few suggestions:

Make clothespin bells by using pipe cleaners to attach jingle bells onto the rounded grooves of craft clothespins.

Make tambourines by placing popcorn inside two paper plates or disposable aluminum pie pans that are then stapled together. For a festive touch, staple lengths of colorful ribbon onto the tambourine when you staple the edges of the plate together.

Glue sandpaper onto small blocks of wood for the children to rub together.

Make noise shakers by placing beans inside tennis ball- or potato chip-cannisters and pennies inside film cans. Secure the lids with strong tape.

Kitchen items are great for rhythm instruments. Tie spoons on lengths of yarn and let children strike them with another spoon, or more simply, let children strike two spoons together. Two old pans can be banged together as cymbals; pots and spoons can become drums. Chopsticks and wooden spoons make good rhythm sticks to be tapped together. A lightweight aluminum cookie sheet can be held in both hands and shaken back and forth to make a sound like thunder.

While rhythm instruments are fun, they can also be distracting to children. Use them with songs the children know well or when you want them just to listen to a new song. Certainly, you don't need to use these instruments every week; rather save them to be used from time to time.

## MOVEMENT GAMES

The movement games are divided into two categories: games that are accompanied by music, and games that are played without music.

The following games are designed to be played with music. You may have children sing or just listen to the song as they do the movements:

### HANDS AND FEET

Here are individual movements that the children can do as they sing or listen to music: clap hands; twirl around; slap knees; hop in place; stamp feet; and raise hands in the air and wiggle fingers. With the help of the children, create other interesting movements.

### CIRCLES

Here are ways that the whole group can move in a circle while singing or listening to music:

Hold hands and walk in a circle.

Form a train by placing hands on the person in front's shoulders or waist and walk in a circle.

Hold hands and swing arms back and forth while standing in a circle.

Hold hands, move to the center, raise arms high, and go back to original places again.

### GOING TO THE HOLY LAND

Place the blanket from the Children's Church Kit on the floor. Explain to the children that they are to pretend the blanket is a magic carpet. When they hear the music play, they are to walk in a circle, stepping on the carpet every time they walk by it. When the music stops, they must freeze. Whoever is standing on the magic carpet when the music stops gets to go and sit in the Holy Land, which is in the center of the circle. When all the children are in the Holy Land, the game is finished.

If you want the game to move along faster, use another blanket or two, or tape several pieces of construction paper to the floor. As children leave the circle to go to the Holy Land, close up the circle so there aren't large gaps between children.

### FROZEN ANGELS

Tell the children that they are angels. They are to fly about however they like when they hear the music playing. When the music stops, they are to freeze in place until the music begins again.

### CHILDREN'S CHURCH KIT

Play musical games using these items from the Children's Church Kit:

Sheet: Spread the sheet on the floor and ask the children to gather around it. When the music starts, they are to pick up the edge of the sheet and shake it in time with the music. For a different twist, place the toy animal from the kit in the center of the sheet and let the children enjoy giving the animal a trampoline ride by shaking the sheet up and down.

Roll up the sheet and place it on the floor. Announce that the sheet is now the River Jordan. Children are to walk in a circle as they sing or listen to the music, "jumping over the Jordan" each time they approach the sheet.

Toy Animal: Have children sit or stand in a circle. While they sing or listen to the music, they are to pass the animal around the circle. If the music is slower in tempo, ask each child to give the animal a hug before passing it on.

Doll: Children may pass the doll around the circle, each taking a moment to cradle the doll in their arms and rock it in time with the music, before passing it on to the next person.

Ball: Children may roll the ball or pass the ball to one another as they sing or listen to the music, or they can play Toe Soccer by sitting in a close circle with their feet extended forward. When the ball comes to them they may flex their feet to send the ball back into the circle. They may not kick or lift their feet or legs off the ground.

### PARADES

Everyone loves a parade! Here are two parade ideas:

Write "Hooray for Children's Church" on paper plates. Children may wave the plates or bang them as they march along.

Play Follow the Leader as you march to music. You can be the first leader to show the children various motions, then others can take a turn. Motions might include: waving, clapping, skipping, wiggling hands in the air, walking with hands on hips, and hopping.

The following movement games are designed to be played without music:

### BIBLE PEOPLE IN MOTION

This game describes Bible characters featured in *Hooray for Children's Church.* Do as many verses as you like each time. Children can follow the motions and listen at first, but soon they will know both words and motions.

I can be Mary rocking Baby Jesus (fold arms and rock back and forth).
I can be Zacchaeus climbing a tree (use arms and legs to pretend to climb).
I can be a child hugging Jesus (cross arms on chest).
I can be Peter fishing in the sea (pretend to cast line and reel in).
I can be Jesus telling a story (gesture with arms).
I can be shepherds watching sheep at night (hand to forehead and look around).
I can be angels singing Jesus' glory (flap arms and pretend to sing).
I can be Hannah praying with all her might (fold hands, bow heads, close eyes).
I can be the younger son marching home (lift knees one at a time to march).
I can be Noah with hammer and saw (pretend to hammer and saw).
I can be Paul preaching in Rome (point finger and shake hand in air).
I can be Lydia hearing God's call (place hand to ear).

### THANK YOU CHARADES

Children can take turns using actions and/or sound effects to act out things for which they are thankful. The other children are to raise their hands to guess the charade. The child acting out the charade will call on children until someone answers correctly. If children have trouble deciding what to act out, you can whisper suggestions in their ears. Here are some ideas: rain, cats, dogs, basketball, ice-cream cones, bicycles, rabbits, frogs, the ocean, books, their church, trees, paints, and bugs.

### CHILDREN'S CHURCH KIT DO AS I DO

Set out the following items from the Children's Church Kit: bell, doll, blanket, and toy animal. Explain to the children that in this game they will take turns being the leader and thinking of actions to do with items from the Children's Church Kit.

Have the children line up. Choose a leader and ask him or her to step out of the line and face the group. Hand the leader an item. After he or she demonstrates an action, the item is passed to the first person in line who uses the object to repeat the action. This continues down the line. Examples: hold the bell high in the air and ring it; make the doll wave its hand; put the blanket on your head and jump up and down; toss the toy animal in the air and catch it.

Change leaders and hand the new leader a different item.

### TRAVELING BIBLE ROADS

Create a winding yarn road on the floor for the children to follow. When you play this game, tell the children that they are one of the following: Paul on his missionary travels; the prodigal son returning home; the wise men looking for Baby Jesus; Joseph and Mary fleeing with the baby to Egypt; or the fishermen disciples following Jesus.

After they have walked the yarn road, give the children some challenging options: walking backward, pretending to walk a tightrope, hopping from one side of the yarn to the other, and walking on tiptoe.

### PASTOR SAYS

Play this liturgical version of Simon Says by giving commands that relate to the worship service: shake hands, stand up, sit down, bow your heads, pass the offering plates, say "Amen," read from the Bible, or open the hymnal.

Appoint an area to be the "choir loft." This is where the children will sit when they are called out.

To play, give a command. If you say "Pastor Says" then the children may do what you ask. If you give a command without first saying "Pastor Says," those who do the command anyway are out. Play until all the children are in the choir loft or time runs short.

## GOD'S WORLD POP-UP

Children are to pop up (stand up) in response to what you say. Encourage them to listen carefully and think before acting. As soon as they stand, they should sit back down again.

Colors: Ask children to stand up if they are wearing the colors you call out. For example: "If you're wearing blue pop up," "If you're wearing brown pop up." Children wearing more than one color will pop up more than once.

Foods: Ask the children to stand up in response to foods. For example: "If you had macaroni and cheese for dinner last night pop up," "If you had toast for breakfast pop up."

Favorites: Ask children to stand up when they hear their favorite season, animal, holiday, or color. It's best to do favorites of one subject at a time. For example: "If your favorite season is spring pop up," "If your favorite season is fall pop up," and "If your favorite color is purple pop up," "If your favorite color is red pop up."

# Section One
## GOD IS LOVE

*"For the LORD is good; his steadfast love endures forever."*
Psalm 100:5

### MESSAGE
God will love us forever.

### OPENING
Music and Movement: Thank You, God, for Loving Me, page 81, *Sing a New Song*

Following Music and Movement, ask the children to sit in a circle.

### SHARING
Ask the children this question: "If you could be any age from a baby to a big kid to a grown-up to a grandparent, what age would you like to be and why?" (I want to be a baby and ride in a stroller; I want to be a grandpa and take kids to the fair; I want to be a teenager so I can drive a car; I want to be a grown-up because I'm going to be a teacher.)

### LISTENING
Begin by saying, "God has loved you since you were a baby and God will love you all the days of your life, no matter what age you are. God's love is forever."

Explain that every time you clap your hands during the following story, the children are to shout, "And God still loved him." Practice this once or twice and then begin:

**Once upon a time, a baby boy was born and God loved him. When he was one he learned to walk (Clap). When he was two he learned to ride a tricycle (Clap). When he was three he learned to brush his teeth (Clap). When he was four he learned to write his name (Clap). When he was five he went to kindergarten and learned to tie his shoes (Clap). When he was six he learned to read (Clap).**

**Before the boy knew it, he was finished with elementary school (Clap). He went to middle school (Clap) and then to high school (Clap). Then he went to college (Clap). Soon he married and had a family (Clap). After his children were grown, they had children. Before he knew it, he was a grandpa (Clap). And through all the days of his life God loved him.**

### PRAYING
Ask the children to close their eyes and bow their heads as you pray:

**Dear God, Thank you for loving us when we were babies and when we were toddlers. Now we're on our way to being big kids and we know that you will love us forever. Amen.**

### EXPLORING
Children will enjoy acting out people of various ages. Let the children give suggestions and the whole group can act them out together.

Begin by saying, "God loved you as babies. What do babies do?" (Cry; crawl; shake rattles; drink from bottles.)

Then say, "God loved you as toddlers. What do toddlers do?" (Toddle about; talk in baby voices; play with their toys.)

Say, "God loves you now. What do you do?" (Ride bikes; eat pizza; brush our teeth; say our prayers.)

Say, "God loves big kids. What do big kids do?" (Cross the street; play basketball; go to slumber parties; do homework and take tests.)

Say, "God loves teenagers. What do teenagers do?" (Drive cars; dance; listen to music; talk on the phone; baby-sit.)

Say, "God loves grown-ups. What do grown-ups do?" (Work at their jobs; cook dinner; fix things that are broken; go shopping.)

Say, "God loves grandparents. What do grandparents do?" (Play with their grandchildren; go on trips; paint; play tennis; bake cookies.)

### SNACKING

Serve a treat that takes a long time to eat such as a candy stick. Tell the children, "These candy sticks take a long time to eat. God's love lasts even longer than these candy sticks. God's love lasts forever!" Encourage kids to lick the candy sticks, not chew them. Send the rest of the stick home wrapped in plastic wrap. Be certain sticky hands are washed.

### MORE EXPLORING

Use the ball from the Children's Church Kit to play Forever Call Ball. Have the children sit down and form a circle. Explain that the person holding the ball is to roll it to someone else saying, "God loves (*name*) forever." That person then rolls the ball to someone else, repeating the phrase but changing the name. To extend the game you can change the phrase and have the children say, "God loved (*name*) as a baby" or "God will love (*name*) as a teenager."

*"God's love lasts even longer than a candy stick."*

# Loving God

*"You shall love the LORD your God with all your heart, and with all your soul, and with all your might."*
*Deuteronomy 6:5*

### MESSAGE
We are to love God.

### OPENING
Music and Movement: The Great Commandments, page 70, *Sing a New Song*

Following Music and Movement, ask the children to sit in a circle.

### LISTENING
Hold up the toy animal from the Children's Church Kit and say, "I'm going to hug this animal with all my might." Then pass the animal around the circle and let each child take a turn giving the animal a big hug. When all have had a turn, begin the story.

**We've just hugged our animal with all our might and shown him (or her) our love. Can you hug God? (No.) We can't actually hug God, but there are other ways to show our love to God.**

**Erin was a little girl about your age. She wanted to love God with all of her might. This is what she did. She went to church and sang the songs with her best singing voice. She listened carefully in Sunday school. All week long she talked to God in her prayers. She thanked God for her family and her dog and she asked God for help whenever she had a problem.**

**Erin also showed God her love by loving others. She drew pictures for her grandpa who was sick. She shared her new bike when her friends came to visit. And even though it wasn't always easy, she tried to be nice to her baby sister.**

**Erin couldn't hug God, but there were lots of ways that she could love God with all of her might. And there are lots of ways that you can love God with all of your might, too!**

### SHARING
Ask the children to each tell one way that they can show love to God. (Going to church; singing songs; praying; helping others; following God's commandments; listening to Bible stories.)

### PRAYER
Say the prayer and show children the motions. Then ask them to join with you as you pray:

**We love you, God, with all our heart (arms crossed gently over chest)**
**And with all our soul (raise hands high above head)**
**And with all our might! (cross arms across chest again, with hands on shoulders, hug tightly)**
**Amen.**

### EXPLORING
Children will make paper heart pendants. To prepare, cut hearts about four inches in diameter from construction paper. Punch a hole in the top of each heart. Cut lengths of yarn about thirty-six inches long, one for each heart.

To begin the activity, say, "To celebrate our love for God, we're going to make heart pendants for you to wear today. When you go to bed you can hang them in your room to remind you that there are lots of ways to show God your love."

Have the children use crayons to decorate the hearts any way they like. When they are finished, help the children thread the pendant with a length of yarn and knot the yarn. After they put the pendants on, tell the children how wonderful they look.

### SNACKING
Serve a snack such as cheese or bread slices that can be cut into a heart shape. Use a heart-shaped cookie cutter or sharp knife to create the heart shape.

### MORE EXPLORING
Send children on a Heart Hunt! To prepare, cut paper hearts about two inches in diameter from construction paper. You will need four or five hearts per child. Hide the hearts around the room.

Just before the Heart Hunt begins, place the basket from the Children's Church Kit in the center of the room. Explain to the children that they are going on a Heart Hunt. They may only pick up one heart at a time. When they find a heart, they must drop it in the basket and say, "I love you God." Then, they may hunt for another heart. When all the hearts have been found, the game is finished.

**OTHER SONGS** from *Sing a New Song*
Down in My Heart, 54
God Loves All Children, 17
Jesus Loves Even Me, 52
Oh, How I Love Jesus, 53

*Heart Hunt*

# God's Son

*"For God so loved the world that he gave his only Son, so that everyone who believes in him may not perish but may have eternal life."*
*John 3:16*

### MESSAGE
God sent his son, Jesus, so that we can have eternal life.

### OPENING
Music and Movement: Oh, How I Love Jesus, page 53, *Sing a New Song*

Following Music and Movement, ask the children to sit in a circle.

### SHARING
Ask the children: "How do you know that your parents love you?" (They take care of me; they tell me that they love me; they give me treats; they hug and kiss me.)

### LISTENING
During the telling of the story, you will cut out three Christian symbols: a heart, a cross, and a butterfly, from three sheets of paper. Fold each sheet of paper in half vertically and practice cutting the symbols as indicated in the diagram.

As you tell the story, cut each symbol and then unfold it.

**We talked about ways that we know that our parents love us. Here is one of the ways we know that God loves us.**

**God loves us so much that two thousand years ago he sent his only son, Jesus, to the earth. (Cut heart and unfold the heart as you talk.)**

**Jesus was born a baby to Mary and Joseph. He grew up to be a man who told lots of people about God. People who didn't like Jesus put him to death by nailing him to a wooden cross. (Cut and unfold the cross as you talk.)**

**Jesus' friends were very sad when he died. They put his body in a tomb. In three days, Jesus rose from the dead. He was alive! Just as a caterpillar**
**comes out of the cocoon as a butterfly, Jesus, who was dead, rose again and came out of the tomb. (Cut and unfold the butterfly as you talk.) This is called the Resurrection.**

**Jesus' death and Resurrection mean that those who believe in him will come to life again after they die on earth. They will go to heaven and live with God.**

### PRAYING
Practice this motion prayer with the children, then say it together:

**Thank you God for loving us so much (hands over head, bent together to form the top of a heart) that you sent Jesus to die on the cross (one arm held straight up from the elbow with the other arm placed horizontally across it to form a cross) and to rise again so that we might have eternal life (hands on hips and arms moving back and forth as butterfly wings). Amen.**

### EXPLORING
The children will color the butterfly from the "Resurrection Butterfly" reproducible. Before you pass the butterflies out say, "Let's celebrate God's love in sending us his son, Jesus, by coloring beautiful butterflies!" When finished, hang the butterflies for decoration or send them home with the children.

### SNACKING
Cut slices of American cheese in half diagonally to form triangles. Show the children how to arrange pretzel sticks and cheese triangles into butterflies. Encourage all to admire their creations before they eat them.

### MORE EXPLORING
Using modeling dough, the children can create three-dimensional shapes of the Christian symbols used in the story: the heart, the cross, and the butterfly. As they work, remind the children of the spiritual significance of the symbols.

**OTHER SONGS** from *Sing a New Song*
Jesus Loves Even Me, 52
Jesus Loves Me, 29
Jesus Loves the Little Children, 27

# Jesus and the Children

*"Let the little children come to me."*
*Matthew 19:14*

### MESSAGE

Jesus loved children and thought that they were special.

### OPENING

Music and Movement: Jesus Loves the Little Children, page 27, *Sing a New Song*

Following Music and Movement, ask the children to sit in a circle.

### SHARING

Have the children each tell about a time when a grown-up made them feel special. (My grandma took me to the circus; my teacher let me hold the flag; my neighbor brought me a birthday present; my dad let me go fishing with him.)

### LISTENING

This is the story of Jesus and the children, based on Matthew 19:13-15:

**It's always fun to feel special. The Bible tells us about a time when Jesus made some children feel very special. Parents brought their children to meet Jesus. They knew that Jesus was an important man. Because they loved their children, they wanted Jesus to lay his hands on their children and to pray for them.**

**Jesus' disciples were standing nearby. They thought that Jesus was too important to be bothered by children. They told the parents to take the children away. Jesus said, "Let the children come to me. Don't stop them. God's kingdom belongs to children, too." And so the children met Jesus and received his blessing.**

**Jesus thought that children were special. Jesus loved children and knew that God loves them too. Let's sing a song about Jesus and children. (Lead the children in singing "Jesus Loves Me.")**

### PRAYING

Ask the children to bow their heads and close their eyes as you pray:

**Dear God, Just as Jesus made the children who met him in the Bible story feel special, we know that all of the children here (name each child) are special too. Thank you! We pray this prayer in the name of Jesus. Amen.**

### EXPLORING

For this activity, children will use crayons to create self-portraits on paper plates. The portraits can then be hung on the wall with masking tape to create a Paper Plate Portrait Gallery.

Introduce the activity by saying, "Jesus loves all of you, even though you are each different. We're going to create a Paper Plate Portrait Gallery. A portrait is a picture of a person. When you draw a portrait of yourself, that's called a 'self-portrait.' Think about what you look like. What color are your eyes? Your skin? Your hair? What shape is your nose? Do you have freckles or wear glasses? Then draw a portrait of yourself on the paper plate."

Be sure to admire the self-portraits as they are completed. Hang them immediately, letting each child select the location on the wall for his or her picture. Over the portraits, hang a sign that says, "Jesus Loves Us."

### SNACKING

Serve a snack that the children who visited Jesus might have enjoyed: grape juice, grapes, raisins, dried figs, and/or pita bread.

### MORE EXPLORING

Have the children act out the story of Jesus and the children. Choose a child to play Jesus and seat him or her in a chair. Choose two or three children to be disciples. Divide the rest of the group into parents and children. Lead children through the story, helping them with lines and actions. If time permits, have the children switch roles and act out the story again.

### OTHER SONGS from *Sing a New Song*
Jesus Loves Even Me, 52
Jesus Loves Me, 29
My Best Friend Is Jesus, 52

# Forgiving

*"Be kind to one another, tenderhearted,*
*forgiving one another,*
*as God in Christ has forgiven you."*
*Ephesians 4:32*

### MESSAGE
God forgives us and wants us to forgive others.

### OPENING
Music and Movement: Forgiveness, page 33, *Sing a New Song*

Following Music and Movement, ask the children to sit in a circle.

### SHARING
Have the children share a time when someone has been unkind to them. (My sister hit me; my cousin said I was stupid; my neighbor kicked over my new bike.)

### PRAYING
Ask the children to close their eyes and bow their heads as you pray:

**Dear God, The Bible says that when we ask you for forgiveness, you forgive us. We can all remember a time when someone has been unkind to us. Help us to forgive other people, just as you forgive us. Amen.**

### LISTENING
Tell the children this story, based on Matthew 18:21-22:

**One day Peter, who was one of Jesus' disciples, asked him, "Jesus, when someone sins against me, how many times should I forgive him? Should I forgive him seven times?"**

**Jesus answered Peter, "You should forgive someone more than seven times. You should forgive him seventy-seven times if he does wrong to you."**

**Jesus tells us that we are to forgive one another over and over and over again. This isn't always easy, but God forgives us and wants us to forgive others.**

### EXPLORING
Children will have a good time playing the Forgiveness Game. This game is less complicated than it sounds, although you will need to lead the children through it to get them started. Warn them that the bumping is just part of the game and is to be done gently!

Divide the group in half. The first half is to form a circle and the second half should form a circle around them. The circles are to face each other. Those on the inside are to gently bump the person opposite them, then say, "Oops, I'm sorry I bumped you!" The person who was bumped says, "I forgive you." The outside circle then rotates one person to the right and the bumping and forgiving begins again. This continues until the entire inside circle has had a turn bumping. The circles can then switch roles with the outside doing the bumping and the inside the forgiving.

If you want to extend the game, play again, with one circle saying something like "You're a creep! Oh, I'm sorry I said that" and the other circle saying, "I forgive you."

### SNACKING
Divide the children into pairs. Explain to them that in centuries gone by, a Forgiveness Cake was shared by two people who had wronged each other and wanted to become friends again. Give each pair a snack cake, graham cracker, or pretzel rod that can be broken in half and shared. Of course the pairs will gladly share seconds and thirds, too!

### MORE EXPLORING
Forgiving Faces is a game that children can learn to play when they actually are angry with someone. Seat the children in pairs, facing one another. Tell them that they are to pretend to be furious at their partner. They are to stare at each other but they must not smile. This is hard to do and will almost always result in smiling faces. Tell them that each time you ring the bell (from the Children's Church Kit), they are to find a new partner. Move the game along until everyone has had a chance to smile with everyone else in the group.

**OTHER SONGS** from *Sing a New Song*

*Sharing*

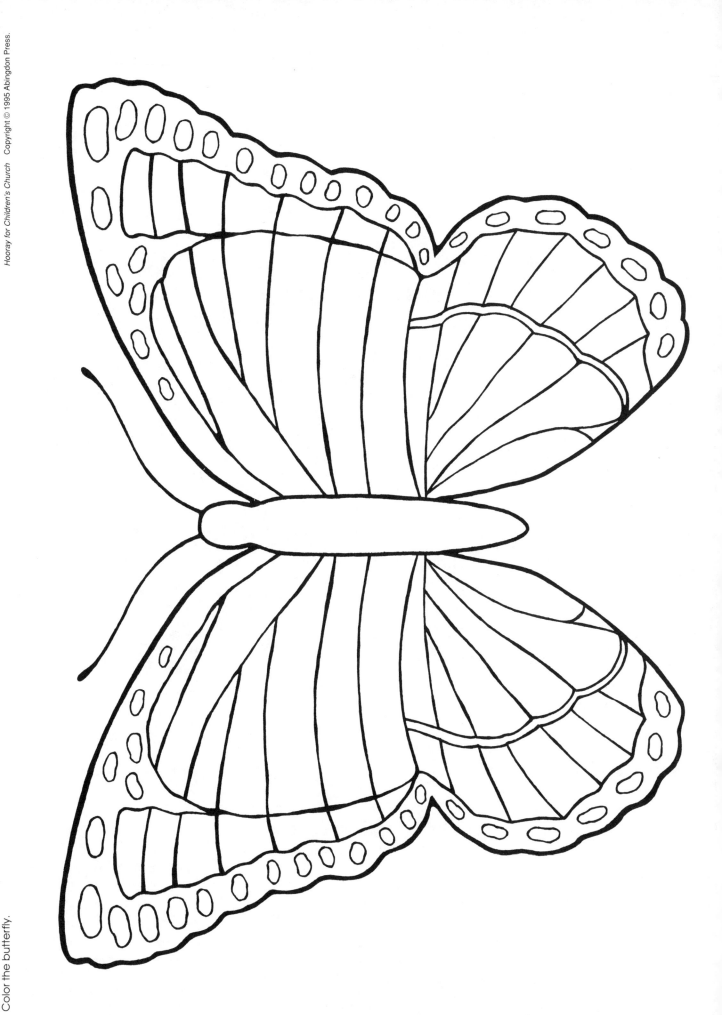

# COME AND WORSHIP

*"I was glad when they said to me,*
*'Let us go to the house of the LORD!'"*
Psalm 122:1

### MESSAGE
We are happy to go to church.

### OPENING
Music and Movement: I Was Glad, page 64, *Sing a New Song*

Following Music and Movement, ask the children to sit in a circle.

### SHARING
Say to the children, "Good Morning! Let me see you smile (pause). Those smiles make your faces look happy! Can you tell me what makes you feel happy?" (Playing with friends; eating ice cream; swimming; my birthday.)

### LISTENING
The children will act out the story by imitating your actions.

**I'll tell you what makes me happy. I feel happy to see all of you at church today. I like to spend time with you here in God's house. Let's pretend that we're getting ready for church! Watch me and then do what I do. Ready?**

**Very early this morning, we were sleeping (rest head to one side on hands and close eyes).**

**It's time to wake up. Open your eyes (stretch arms and yawn).**

**Next we get out of bed and eat breakfast (stand up, walk in place, then sit back down and pretend to eat).**

**After breakfast we wash our faces (rub hands on cheeks); brush our teeth (pretend to brush); and get dressed (pretend to button a shirt).**

**Oops! Don't forget to comb your hair (pretend to comb hair).**

**Now we're ready for church. Some of us walk to church (walk in place); some of us ride a bus or subway (reach one arm up and close hand as if grasping a rail); some of us ride in a car (sit down and pretend to buckle a seat belt).**

**Did anyone ride a bike (seated, raise feet and pedal in circular motion)? Did anyone roller-skate to church (seated, slide feet up and back)?**

**Whew! We are finally at church and we greet our friends (wave; shake hands). All the people here at church pray to God (fold hands and bow heads); we sing praises to God (hold hands like a book and pretend to sing); and listen to God's word (hand cupped to one ear).**

**We're glad to come to God's house!**

### PRAYING
Ask the children to bow their heads and close their eyes as you pray:

**Thank you, God, for our church. We are happy to be here praying and praising, singing and listening. Amen.**

### EXPLORING
Sing the "Come to Church Song" to the tune of "If You're Happy and You Know It." Add simple motions.

Verse 1: If you're happy and you know it (cross arms across chest with hands on shoulders, as if hugging yourself) come to church (raise hands over heads, touching fingertips to form a steeple),

If you're happy and you know it (hug self) come to church (hands form steeple),

If you're happy and you know it (hug self), then God will also know it (raise one arm and point upward),

If you're happy and you know it (hug self) come to church.

Verse 2: If you're happy and you know it (hug self) pray to God (fold hands).

Verse 3: If you're happy and you know it (hug self) hear God's word (cup hand to ear).

Verse 4: If you're happy and you know it (hug self) sing a hymn (hold hands like book).

Verse 5: If you're happy and you know it (hug self) bring a friend (link arms with a partner).

Verse 6: If you're happy and you know it (hug self) shout "HOORAY" (shout hooray and jump up and down).

### SNACKING

The children can use tubed frosting to draw Sweet Steeples on graham crackers. Demonstrate by drawing a rectangle on the cracker and adding a triangular steeple.

### MORE EXPLORING

Make a simple line drawing of your church on a length of shelf or craft paper. Invite the children to create a Come to Church Mural by drawing themselves with crayon, coming to church.

### OTHER SONGS from *Sing a New Song*

We're Going to Our Church, 30

Jesus Is Calling, 66

This Little Light of Mine, 67

---

# Praising God

*"He entered the temple with them, walking and leaping and praising God." Acts 3:8*

### MESSAGE

We come to church to praise God.

### OPENING

Music and Movement: Praise God, page 47, *Sing a New Song*

Following Music and Movement, ask the children to sit in a circle.

### PRAYING

Say a responsive Alleluia Prayer with the children by speaking a line of the prayer, then clapping your hands once. Ask the children to answer your clap with a clap of their own and with a shout of "Alleluia!"

God of Glory, (you clap, children respond) your name we praise (clap, response). We love you (clap, response). We come to worship you (clap, response). We praise your greatness (clap, response). Amen.

### SHARING

Say to the children, "Can you show me how you look when you feel excited and happy?" (Pause while the children smile, laugh, or jump up and down.) Then say, "That's great! You certainly look excited and happy. Today we're going to hear a happy story about a man who praised God by jumping and leaping."

### LISTENING

The story is based on Acts 3:1-10:

**A beggar sat every day at the Beautiful Gate, outside the temple. The poor beggar had never been able to walk. People helped the man by carrying him to the gate where he begged for money.**

One day two disciples of Jesus, Peter and John, came to the temple to pray. They saw the beggar and wanted to help him, too. They asked the man to look at them. The beggar looked at them, expecting some money. But Peter said that he didn't have gold or silver to give the man; instead he had a gift to give the beggar in the name of Jesus Christ of Nazareth. Peter said, "Stand up and walk." Then he helped the man stand. Suddenly, the beggar's feet and ankles were healed and made strong. The man who had never walked began to walk! He was so excited that he went to the temple walking and leaping and praising God. All the people who knew the beggar were filled with amazement and wonder when they saw him.

### EXPLORING

Before Children's Church, assemble the "We Praise God" booklets. First, make one copy of the reproducible for each child. Next, fold along the #1 fold line (the longest), with the pictures facing outward. Then, fold on the #2 fold line. The booklet is now ready for the children to color.

After the booklets are finished, you may want to put two staples along the #2 fold line to make it seem more like a book.

### SNACKING

Throwing brightly colored confetti is a festive way to celebrate an occasion. Serve this colorful Confetti Snack and explain to the children what it represents.

Place several of the following foods in separate bowls: grated cheese, grated carrots, coconut (can be colored with food coloring), chow mein noodles; or colored cereal. Children will enjoy eating the snack with their fingers.

### MORE EXPLORING

Play the Praise God Leapabout and let the children praise God! Have everyone stand in a wide circle, with space between children. Explain to the children that they are going to play a leaping game by taking turns around the circle. When it is their turn they are to make a big leap into the circle and praise God for a part of their body (eyes, ears, fingers, freckles, knees) saying, "I praise God for my _____." To help the children take turns, they will all clap their hands three times and say, "Clap, clap, clap for (*child's name*)" and that child will leap in. When the child leaps back again, everyone is to clap three times again and say the next child's name. Demonstrate by clapping, saying your own name, leaping, praising God, leaping back, clapping, and naming the child to your right.

**OTHER SONGS** from *Sing a New Song*
Alleluia, 53
Happy All the Time, 94
The Things We Need, 92

*Confetti Snack*

# Listening at Church

*"They found him in the temple, sitting among the teachers, listening to them and asking them questions."*
*Luke 2:46*

### MESSAGE
We can listen at church, like Jesus did.

### OPENING
Music and Movement: Jesus Learned About God, page 23, *Sing a New Song*

Following Music and Movement, ask the children to sit in a circle.

### SHARING
Ask the children to tell something that they hear at church (music; Bible stories; prayers). Encourage them to listen carefully as each person speaks, and tell them that you have on your listening ears, too.

### LISTENING
Read the story of Jesus at the Temple directly from the Bible (Luke 2:41-52). Explain that Jewish people worship in a temple, not a church. Follow the scripture reading with these questions designed to build understanding:

**When Jesus and his parents went to the festival in Jerusalem, how old was Jesus? (Twelve.)**

**How far away were Jesus' parents before they missed him? (A day's journey.)**

**Where was Jesus when they found him? (In the temple.)**

**What was Jesus doing at the temple? (Listening to teachers and asking questions.)**

**Were his parents upset with him? (Yes.)**

**Jesus asked his parents, "Didn't you know that I was in my Father's house?" Did he mean his father Joseph's house in Nazareth, or God's house? (God's house.)**

**Did Jesus obey his parents and go back to Nazareth with them? (Yes.)**

Conclude by emphasizing that Jesus listened carefully at the temple and he also listened to his parents.

### PRAYING
Ask the children to close their eyes and bow their heads as you pray:

**Great God who hears our prayers, We will try to be good listeners at church and at home. Amen.**

### EXPLORING
Children will play the listening game, Jump for Jesus. You will say names, then say "Jesus," then continue saying names, interspersing "Jesus" as often as you wish. Ask the children to listen carefully and jump up when they hear the name Jesus. After they jump up, they should sit down again and continue listening carefully. For example: Ben, Laura, Drew, Katherine, Henry, Emily, Adam, JESUS, Louise, Chris, Mary, JESUS, Beth, Daniel, Ashley, Josh, JESUS, Sarah. . . .

### SNACKING
There's no better snack for listening ears than popcorn. Cook the popcorn in front of the children and challenge them to listen for the first pop and the last!

### MORE EXPLORING
In this game, Listen for the Church Bell, the children are to form a circle. One child is chosen to be the Listener. The Listener goes to the middle of the circle and closes his or her eyes. Next, hand the bell from the Children's Church Kit (hold the clapper) to one of the children. This child, the Church Bell, will ring the bell three or four times. Then the Listener will try to walk to the Church Bell without looking. Try to give each child an opportunity to be the Listener and the Church Bell.

**OTHER SONGS** from *Sing a New Song*
Come! Come! Everybody Worship! 31
Jesus Saw the Flowers, 24
We're Going to Our Church, 30

# Singing to God

*"With gratitude in your hearts sing psalms, hymns, and spiritual songs to God."*
Colossians 3:16

### MESSAGE
We worship God with singing.

### OPENING
Music and Movement: Sing for Joy! page 50, *Sing a New Song*

Following Music and Movement, ask the children to sit in a circle.

### SHARING
Ask the children to each say the name of one of their favorite church songs and if they seem willing, to sing a line of the song. ("Zacchaeus"; "Jesus Loves Me"; "Away in a Manger.")

### PRAYING
Introduce the prayer by saying, "We worship God with our songs. We do this when we sing about Bible stories, when we sing about the beautiful earth God created, when we sing songs of praise and thanks, and we can also sing our prayers." Sing the prayer for the children, then sing it together. (To the tune of "Row, Row, Row Your Boat.")

**We sing, sing, sing to God,**
**Sing with all our hearts.**
**Sing at church and sing at home,**
**We sing with all our hearts.**

### LISTENING
Share this story about a boy who liked to sing at church:

**This is a story about a boy named Matthew who liked to sing.**

**The first time Matthew came to the big church, he was just a baby, two months old. His mother thought that he was too little for the nursery so she held him in her arms. When the worshipers** were singing a hymn, Matthew began to gurgle and coo. People turned to look at him and smiled.

A year later, Matthew came to worship again, during a special Christmas service. When people started singing, Matthew sang too, "Da-da-da-da!" After the service, people told Matthew's mother that they enjoyed his singing.

When Matthew was about your age, he went to a baby's baptism. Everyone sang "Jesus Loves Me." Matthew sang along too because he knew the words. Later the people sang another song. Matthew didn't know the words to this song but since he liked to sing, he sang "La-la-la-la." He sang loudly and his mother shook her head at him. After church, Reverend Taylor said to him, "I'm glad to hear you worship God with your singing." His mother smiled.

A few years later, Matthew was old enough to go to big church. He was happy because now he could read and sing the hymns like the grown-ups. When a song had a hard word in it he would sing "hum, hum."

The year that Matt, which is what everyone called him then, went into the sixth grade, the choir director said, "I've known you since you were a baby and you've always liked to sing. Would you like to be a member of the Youth Choir?" Matt smiled and sang, "Yes!"

### EXPLORING
Children will make Paper Bag Puppets that they will use to act out Matthew's singing in the story.

To make the puppets, you'll need for each child: a luncheon size paper bag, glue, crayons, and pre-cut construction paper to make eyes, mouth, and hair.

For the eyes, cut circles about the size of a quarter from white paper. Use pink or red paper to cut one two-inch circle for each puppet's mouth. To make hair, cut strips of yellow, brown, and black construction paper about five inches long.

To begin, ask the children to take two white circles and color their eye color in the middle of each circle. With the bag flat on the table and the folded side up, glue the two eyes to the center of the bottom of the bag. Next, hand a mouth to each child. Tell them to glue the mouths in the fold at the bottom of the bag. Have children select the hair color most similar to theirs and glue the strips around the outside edges of the bottom of the bag. The strips can be torn to make bangs or short hair and curled around a crayon to make curly hair.

The paper bag puppets are ready to sing! Have the children slip their hands into the open end of the bag with their fingers in the fold of the bag and their thumbs under the mouth so the puppets' mouths can move.

Lead the children through the Listening story, having them sing as Matthew did as he was growing.

### SNACKING

Serve an "O"-shaped cereal. Ask the children what shape their mouths make when they sing.

They'll realize mouths make an "O" shape, just like the snack!

### MORE EXPLORING

Play tapes of familiar church songs and let the children use their puppets to sing along, or take the children with their puppets to the church nursery to sing for the babies and toddlers.

**OTHER SONGS** from *Sing a New Song*
Come! Come! Everybody Worship! 31
Sing a Song of Praise, 62
This Is the Day, 63

---

# Praying at Church

*"Pray then in this way: Our Father in heaven, hallowed be your name."*
*Matthew 6:9*

### MESSAGE

We pray at church the prayer that Jesus taught.

### OPENING

Music and Movement: Thank You, God, for Loving Me, page 81, *Sing a New Song*

Following Music and Movement, ask the children to sit in a circle.

### SHARING

Ask the children, "Can you show me what people look like when they pray?" (Eyes closed; hands folded; heads bowed.) Then ask, "Do you remember who showed you how to pray?" (My mother; my grandpa; my father; my Sunday school teacher.)

### LISTENING

Tell children a simple explanation of the prayer that Jesus taught, the Lord's Prayer (Matthew 6:9-15).

The Bible tells us that Jesus taught his followers how to pray. Jesus told them that God does not want to hear fancy words. Jesus explained that God understands what we need. He said that forgiving other people is important. He told his followers to forgive people who hurt them or made them angry. God will forgive the bad things you do if you can forgive others.

We call the prayer that Jesus taught his followers "The Lord's Prayer." Every time we say The Lord's Prayer, we are praising God, asking God to take care of us, and asking God to forgive us as we promise to forgive others.

### PRAYING

Tell children that some people like to pray on their knees. Ask them to kneel, close their eyes, and bow their heads. Pray The Lord's Prayer as it is said in your church or read the excerpt from Matthew.

### EXPLORING

Praying Plates are a mealtime prayer reminder for the children to take home. You'll need paper plates, yarn, old magazines, glue, hole punch, scissors, and crayons. Depending on the capabilities of your group, you may wish to do some preparation beforehand.

To make a Prayer Plate, punch two holes about four inches apart on one edge of the plate. Tie each end of a fifteen-inch length of yarn at the holes. Write "Give us this day our daily bread" around the rim of the plate.

The children will look through old magazines to find a picture of a favorite food. They are to cut out the picture and glue it to the center of the plate.

Remind the group that the words "Give us this day our daily bread" are from the prayer that Jesus taught, The Lord's Prayer. Suggest that the plate be hung in the kitchen or dining room at home to remind families at mealtime to thank God for their food.

### SNACKING

Serve pretzels twisted into the traditional pretzel shape. A legend tells of a fifth-century monk who created pretzels to encourage children to pray. The children of that time folded their arms across their chests (hands on opposite shoulder) when they prayed. Ask your children to cross their arms like the children of long ago, then serve them pretzels twisted into the shape of praying arms.

### MORE EXPLORING

This Prayer Parade can be done standing still at first, then as a march when the children catch on:

Leader: **Step, step; clap, clap; can we bow our heads to pray?**

All: **Step, step; clap, clap; we can bow our heads to pray!**

Leader: **Step, step; clap, clap; can we close our eyes to pray?**

All: **Step, step; clap, clap; we can close our eyes to pray!**

Other verses:
**Can we fold our hands to pray?**
**Can we stand up and pray?**
**Can we sit down and pray?**
**Can we hold hands to pray?**
**Can we come to church to pray?**
**Can we be at home and pray?**

**OTHER SONGS** from *Sing a New Song*
I'm Thankful for My Senses, 89
My Feet Stand, 62
The Things We Need, 92

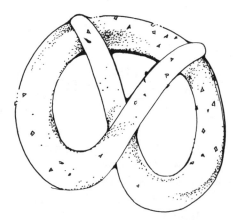

# Building the Church

*"You are Peter, and on this rock
I will build my church."*
Matthew 16:18

### MESSAGE
The church is built by people.

### OPENING
Music and Movement: We're Going to Our Church, page 30, *Sing a New Song*

Following Music and Movement, ask the children to sit in a circle.

### SHARING
Take the rock from the Children's Church Kit and hold it up for all to see. Tell the children that you are going to pass the rock around the circle. When each child receives the rock, he or she will name something that is built with rocks. (Walls; castles; roads; churches; houses.)

### LISTENING
Place the rock on your lap while you read this true story:

I think rocks like this one could be used to build a church. Some churches around the world are made with rough rocks, some are made with smooth rocks, and some are made with rocks that have been cut into blocks. I don't think that rocks can make themselves into a church, do you? (No.) How do rocks become churches? (People use them to build churches.) Can people have a church without a special building? Listen to this true story and then tell me your answer.

A few years ago, a little town woke up smelling smoke. When the people of the town saw the smoke and heard the crackling and roaring of flames, they realized that a building must be on fire. Quickly the firefighters and the townspeople found the fire. It was in a very old church.

The brave firefighters broke in the doors and carried in their great water hoses to flood the flames and cool the ashes. Soon, the church members came to see their damaged church. Many of them cried. Some of the people were so upset that all they could do was sit and stare at their burned church.

Since the church was built with rocks cut into big blocks, the fire could not make the church fall down. The fire burned through floors and books and chairs. It melted tables and toys and telephones. The fire made the church black and it smelled terrible. The church people thought that they could fix their church, but they knew it would be a while before they could use the building again.

The church people said to each other, "We can still meet for Sunday school and worship. The church is not a building, it's really the people who are the church."

The next Sunday after the fire, they used smoky hymnals and folding chairs and sat under the trees of the church yard for worship.

Did the people in the story need a building in order to worship as a church? (No.) They just needed to be together.

A long time ago, Jesus said to his disciple, Peter, "You are Peter, and on this rock I will build my church." Jesus wanted Peter to help him build the Christian Church. Jesus did not think that Peter was a real rock to build a church with, but Jesus wanted Peter to tell others about him and to help begin the Christian Church. Jesus knew that people who believe in him and meet together as Christians make a church.

### PRAYING
Invite the children to stand up and come close to you as you hold the rock. Ask everyone to place a finger on the rock, then close their eyes as you pray:

Lord of all people, We meet together in this place because we believe in you. Thank you for sending Jesus to lead and teach us. Thank you for Peter and all the people who build churches. Amen.

### EXPLORING
This activity uses the modeling dough from the Children's Church Kit. Before Children's Church,

cut index cards in half lengthwise and then cut each half into three rectangles. From the rectangles cut small crosses.

To begin the activity, announce to the children that you are going to give them a "rock." Give each child a lump of modeling dough. Ask them to turn their modeling dough rocks into churches. After the churches are built, give them each a white cross to decorate their church.

### SNACKING

Serve Church Rock Pudding. Prepare enough instant or cooked pudding to give everyone a dollop in a paper cup. Purchase a variety of interesting "rocks" such as miniature marshmallows, small, colored candies, or raisins. Pour the rocks into separate bowls and allow the children to mix their favorites into the pudding.

### MORE EXPLORING

Take the children on a guided tour of the church. They will be interested in closets and furnace rooms, bell pulls and plaques, the kitchen and the choir room. They may especially enjoy a good look at the older kids' Sunday school rooms. Add tidbits of information such as "Katie's dad built those bookshelves," or "This is where we keep the costumes for the pageant."

**OTHER SONGS** from *Sing a New Song*
If I Had a Drum, 28
We Are Messengers, 32
We Love, 72

*Church Rock Pudding*

We praise God
for animals.

4

3

We praise God for our friends.

FOLD LINE #2

FOLD LINE # 1

WE PRAISE

GOD

We praise
God for
our church.

To make booklet, fold on dotted lines. *WE PRAISE GOD* will be the cover. Color.

2

## Good Friends

*"A friend loves at all times."*
*Proverbs 17:17*

### MESSAGE
The Bible tells us to be a good friend.

### OPENING
Music and Movement: A Friend Is a Wonderful Thing, page 84, *Sing a New Song*

Following Music and Movement, ask the children to sit in a circle.

### SHARING
Ask each child to tell the group the name of a friend. Jot down the names to be used in the prayer.

### LISTENING
Before Children's Church, draw happy and sad faces on paper plates, one plate for each child.

Begin the story:

**There is a verse in the Bible that says, "A friend loves at all times." God wants us to try and be kind to our friends all of the time. Sometimes, this isn't easy. (Give each child a paper plate.) Listen as I tell you about friends. When someone is being a good friend, hold up the happy face so I can see it. When someone is being a bad friend, hold up the sad face.**

**Jason's friend, Randall, was sick. Jason brought him a coloring book (good friend).**

**Maria was so angry at Heather for breaking her magic wand that she slapped her (bad friend).**

**Andrea told Tim that he was stupid (bad friend).**

**Laura and Corbin took turns on the swing (good friend).**

**David knocked over Tonya's block tower (bad friend).**

**Yolanda invited her new friend, Stephanie, to Children's Church (good friend).**

**Kim tore up the picture Lilly painted (bad friend).**

**Troy gave Chase half of his ice-cream sandwich (good friend).**

**Beth and Amy took turns listening through the headphones (good friend).**

### PRAYING
Have the children hand you the paper plates. They may take them home, if they like, when Children's Church is over. Ask them to bow their heads and close their eyes for a prayer:

**Dear God, We know that it isn't easy to be kind to our friends all of the time, but please help us to try. We want to be good friends to one another and to (read list of names from Sharing). Amen.**

### EXPLORING
Children will make two friendship bracelets, one for themselves and one to give to a friend.

Before Children's Church, cut four-by-six-inch index cards in half lengthwise, then cut each length into one-inch rectangles. Punch two holes at each end of each rectangle. Cut lengths of yarn eight inches long. Thread the yarn through the holes at each end of the rectangles and knot the yarn.

After explaining to the children that friendship bracelets are a fun way to help us think about our friends, invite them to decorate the bracelets using foil stars and crayons. When they are finished, help the children tie the bracelets to their wrists. Remind them to give their other bracelet to a friend.

### SNACKING
The children will have a great time squirting tubed icing onto sugar cookies to create the happy faces of their friends.

37

## MORE EXPLORING

Demonstrate how to play this handshaking game, then help the children find partners.

I'm (*both partners say their names*), I'm your friend (shake right hands, then left),

Let's high five (slap each other's hands, high in the air),

Then let's bend (both partners bend at the knees),

Let's turn around (stand and both spin around),

And shake again (shake right hands, then left),

I'm very glad to be your friend (place hands on each other's shoulders).

Children may play the handshaking game again with this partner, then switch the partners around and continue playing as time permits.

## MORE SONGS from *Sing a New Song*

Having Fun Today, 91
Welcome, Friend, 85
Love One Another, 82
Happy Friends, 83

---

# Love Your Neighbor

*"You shall love your neighbor as yourself."*
*Leviticus 19:18*

### MESSAGE
God wants us to love our neighbors.

### OPENING
Music and Movement: Love Your Neighbor, page 82, *Sing a New Song*

Following Music and Movement, ask the children to sit in a circle.

### LISTENING
Say to the children:

**In the days of the Old Testament, long before Jesus was born, God gave us a set of laws called "The Ten Commandments." These are rules that help us know how God wants us to behave. One of the commandments is "You shall love your neighbor as yourself." Even though a neighbor is usually someone who lives near you, many Christians feel that God meant that we should love everyone, near or far. Today, let's just think about those people who live near to us and how we can show them that we love and care for them.**

### SHARING
Ask the children to each say the name of a neighbor and one way that they could show that person or family God's love. (I can visit; I can bring flowers from our garden; I can be nice to the toddler next door; my dad and I will invite them for a cookout.)

### PRAYING
Ask the children to put their own hands together with their fingertips touching high above their heads. Tell them they look just like houses in a neighborhood! Ask them to close their eyes while you pray:

**Almighty God, Help us to be good neighbors.
Amen.**

## EXPLORING

For this activity you will need the following items from the Children's Church Kit: the sheet, the toy animal, the doll, the blanket, the bell, the basket, the rock, and the ball. You may hold up the items or let the children take turns holding them up, although there won't be an item for everyone. As the item is held up, read the corresponding situation and ask, "What would a good neighbor do?" Remind children that they should never leave their own home or yard without checking with a grown-up first.

Sheet: This sheet has fallen off your neighbor's clothesline. (Hang it back up; tell the neighbor.)

Ball: A new child has moved in next door. (Invite him or her to play catch.)

Doll wrapped in blanket: A neighbor just had a new baby. (Make her a card; help your mother fix her a meal; take the baby a present.)

Toy animal: The little girl in the house behind yours is sitting outside, crying. (Bring your animal to comfort her; share your animal and suggest a game.)

Basket: A man in your neighborhood is sick. (Help prepare a meal to take to him and deliver it in the basket; bring flowers in the basket.)

Bell: The phone rings and you answer it. It is the elderly woman who lives down the street. (Say "Hello, how are you?" politely ask her to hold for a moment while you get your mother or father.)

Rock: The family next door is digging a garden but the soil is filled with rocks. (Help them dig out the rocks; carry the rocks to a bucket for them.)

## SNACKING

Show kids how to arrange pretzel sticks into the shape of houses. After they have created a pretzel neighborhood, invite the children to enjoy the pretzels.

## MORE EXPLORING

Stretch children out in a line to play the Hello Neighbor game. Children are to bend one arm at the elbow with palm facing outward. The game begins when the first child in line knocks on the palm of the second child and says, "Hello neighbor. Let's play." The first child then puts his or her hands on the second child's waist. Together they move on to the third child. The second child knocks on the third child and says, "Hello neighbor. Let's play." This continues until all the children have been invited to play. Break the children apart, ask them to switch their places around, and play again.

**MORE SONGS** from *Sing a New Song*
Love One Another, 82
The Family of God, 80
Welcome, Friend, 85

*Pretzel House*

# Jesus Made Friends

*"I have called you friends, because I have made known to you everything that I have heard from my Father."*
*John 15:15*

### MESSAGE
Jesus made friends with people he met.

### OPENING
Music and Movement: Zacchaeus, page 71, *Sing a New Song*

Following Music and Movement, ask the children to sit in a circle.

### SHARING
Ask the children to tell about a time when they made a friend. (I met a new girl at school; on vacation I played with a boy I met in the next cabin; when Chelsea moved in next door, we became friends.)

### LISTENING
Tell the story of Zacchaeus from Luke 19:1-10:

**Jesus made friends with lots of people. He wanted them to realize that he was God's son and to tell them about God. Often he made friends with people that other people thought were bad. There was a man named Zacchaeus who was a tax collector. He took money from people.**

**Zacchaeus heard that Jesus was coming to his town and he wanted to see him. Zacchaeus wasn't very tall so he climbed up in a sycamore tree to get a better view of Jesus. When Jesus came by he saw Zacchaeus in the tree and said, "Zacchaeus, hurry and come down; for I must stay at your house today." The people who saw this began to grumble and say, "Why, he is going to the house of a sinner!"**

**Even though Zacchaeus was a bad man, Jesus wanted to visit him. Zacchaeus climbed out of the sycamore tree and took Jesus to his house. He promised Jesus that he would pay back the money he took. Zacchaeus believed that Jesus was the son of God.**

If children know the Bible song, "Zacchaeus," sing it with them. If they don't know it, this is a fine time to teach it to them. The song is included on page 71 of *Sing a New Song*.

### PRAYING
Ask children to stand up and hold their arms high in the air. They're trees! Ask them to keep this pose as you teach them this prayer, then pray it together:

**Dear God,
Thanks for trees and thanks for me,
Thanks for Jesus who made friends with
   Zacchaeus. Amen.**

### EXPLORING
Children will use paper, crayons, and glue to create a picture of Zacchaeus in the tree. Each child will need one sheet of white paper, ½ sheet of green construction paper, and a strip of brown paper about four-by-two inches long. Have children glue the brown tree trunk to the bottom half of the white paper. Next, ask them to draw a circle a few inches above the tree trunk and turn it into the face of Zacchaeus. Next, show them how to tear the green paper into somewhat round pieces to be the leaves of the tree. Have them glue the leaves around the head of Zacchaeus and around the top of the tree trunk. Now they have a picture of Zacchaeus peeking out from the sycamore tree!

### SNACKING
Fresh or frozen broccoli spears make perfect trees. Children may enjoy dipping their trees into melted cheese, ranch dressing, or an herb dip.

### MORE EXPLORING
Have the children make leaf rubbings using leaves, white paper, and crayons. If weather permits, the children will enjoy gathering the leaves themselves.

**OTHER SONGS** from *Sing a New Song*
If I Had a Drum, 28
Jesus Loves Me, 29
Love One Another, 82

# Church Friends

*"Greet the friends there,
each by name."*
3 John 1:15

### MESSAGE

The people at church are our friends.

### OPENING

Music and Movement: The Family of God, page 80, *Sing a New Song*

Following Music and Movement, ask the children to sit in a circle.

### SHARING

Ask each child to name someone at church who is their friend. Remind them that grown-ups at church are our friends, too.

### LISTENING

Invite a teenager or adult friend in the congregation to visit Children's Church. Ask this special guest to read a picture book, show the church scrapbook or videos of church events, or talk about the church and its history, mission, and traditions. When you invite the guest, remind him or her of the short but enthusiastic attention spans of children this age.

Explain to the children that today one of their many older friends at church has come as a special guest. Give the guest a hearty introduction and ask the children to say, "Welcome (*name*) to Children's Church." Encourage the children to ask the guest questions after he or she has made the presentation.

### PRAYING

Invite the children and the guest to join you in holding hands around the circle. Ask them to close their eyes and bow their heads as you pray:

**Dear God, We're happy that our church friend, (name), could visit Children's Church today. Thank you for our church and all of our church friends. Amen.**

### EXPLORING

Children enjoy hearing their names in songs. To the tune of "For He's a Jolly Good Fellow" sing the lyrics below. To determine who's name to put into the song, walk around the circle and put your hand on a child's head. Move randomly about the circle until everyone has had a chance to be "The Jolly Good Church Friend."

**For (*name*) is a jolly good church friend,
(*Name*) is a jolly good church friend,
(*Name*) is a jolly good church friend,
We're glad that we're all friends!**

If time permits, let the children give the names of other church members such as the pastor and their Sunday school teachers, and add their names to the song.

### SNACKING

The early Christian friends shared meals together, often eating from the same serving bowl and dipping into the food with flat bread. Make Friendly Whip according to the recipe below, or a bowl of pudding, and let the children scoop it up with graham crackers. Break the graham crackers into smaller sections and remind the children not to dip a cracker that they have bitten from back into the bowl.

To make Friendly Whip: Stir 1½ cups boiling water into two 3-ounce packages of flavored gelatin. Then add 1½ cups of cold water and stir. Chill until thick. Beat in one 8-ounce package non-dairy whipped topping. Chill again until time to serve.

When the fun is over, wash sticky hands.

### MORE EXPLORING

Toward the close of the worship service, perhaps during the final hymn, take the children into the big church to see all of their church friends. Depending on the layout of your church, you may want to sit children on the front steps to face the congregation, in the aisles, or in the balcony. At the close of the service, children may stand with the pastor to shake hands with their many friends at church.

**OTHER SONGS** from *Sing a New Song*

# Friends Across the World

*"Go therefore and make disciples of all nations, baptizing them in the name of the Father and of the Son and of the Holy Spirit."*
Matthew 28:19

## MESSAGE
We have Christian friends all over the world.

## OPENING
Music and Movement: Forgiveness, page 33, *Sing a New Song*

Following Music and Movement, ask the children to sit in a circle.

## SHARING
Ask the children to each name a faraway place.

## LISTENING
Spread the sheet in a different location in the room and invite the children to sit on it. If this isn't practical, ask them to stand while you spread out the sheet and then invite them to sit down on it. Begin the story by saying:

**You may think that you are sitting on an old sheet. Actually, you're sitting on a magic carpet. We'll be leaving for a magic carpet ride in just a moment. First listen carefully.**

**Before Jesus rose into heaven, he told his disciples, "Go therefore and make disciples of all nations, baptizing them in the name of the Father and of the Son and of the Holy Spirit." Jesus wanted those who believed in him to tell others. This is how the church spread across the world. There are now Christian churches all over the world. As we pretend to fly on our magic carpet, let's wave to our Christian friends in those churches. Ready? Here we go!**

**We're already over South America. Let's wave to the Christian friends who live here. (Everyone pretend to look down and wave.)**

**Now we're flying over Africa. Let's shout hello to these Christian friends. (Cup hands to mouth and shout hello.)**

**Here's Europe. Don't lean over too far, you might fall out, but let's shout "Greetings from Children's Church in (*name your town and state*)." (Cup hands to mouth and shout greetings.)**

**Right now we're looking down on Christian friends in India. Let's wave to them. (Look down and wave.)**

**Gee, this magic carpet is fast. We're over Australia already! Let's shout "Hello friends" to these Australian Christians. (Cup hands to mouth and shout "Hello friends.")**

**Well, we're almost home. (Pause.) The magic carpet is about to land. (Pause.) Here we are back at our own church in (*name your town and state*). It's great to be home but wasn't it fun seeing Christian friends all across the world?**

## PRAYING
Say, "Let's pray in another language this morning as we thank God for Christian friends all over the world. First I'll say the prayer in English, then in Spanish. Bow your heads and close your eyes as I pray:

**God of all nations, Thank you for Christian friends all over the world. Amen.**

**Dios de todos los países, Le damos gracias por nuestros amigos cristianos en todo el mundo. Amén.**

## EXPLORING
Hand each child a copy of the "Friends Across the World" reproducible. Ask the children to color the globe, then cut it out. Glue or staple each globe to a paper plate, punch a hole in the top, and tie on a loop of yarn. Tell the children to hang their globes in their rooms to remind them they have Christian friends living all over the world.

## SNACKING
Serve an international snack such as tortilla chips and salsa, or french bread and cheese.

## MORE EXPLORING
Play Follow the Leader, a game that is played by children all across the world. Explain that even

though the world's children often live in very different places, they like to play many of the same games. Eskimo children even play Follow the Leader in the snow!

Let the children take turns being the leader. You may want to give leaders suggestions as to where they might lead the group: cutting a path through a dense jungle; marching across deep snow; paddling a canoe along a dangerous river; walking across hot sand dunes; wading through a marsh; hiking over steep mountains; navigating about a crowded city; or strolling across the countryside.

**OTHER SONGS** from *Sing a New Song*

Color and cut out picture.  Glue to paper plate.

## Advent

*"A voice cries out: 'In the wilderness prepare the way of the LORD, make straight in the desert a highway for our God.' "*
Isaiah 40:3

### MESSAGE

Advent is the time we prepare to celebrate Jesus' birth.

### OPENING

Music and Movement: March, page 87, *Sing a New Song*

Following Music and Movement, ask the children to sit in a circle.

### PRAYING

Have the children bow their heads and close their eyes as you read the prayer:

**Dear God,**
**In the weeks before Christmas Day,**
**We do many things to prepare the way.**
**We pray and sing and listen to stories,**
**That tell of Jesus' birth and of your glory.**
**This season of joy is called "Advent,"**
**As we get ready for the gift you sent.**
**Your son, Jesus, who was laid in a manger,**
**Was visited and honored by many a stranger.**
**We, too, honor Jesus and celebrate his birth,**
**As believers do all over the earth. Amen.**

### SHARING

Tell the children that Advent is the four weeks before Christmas. This is the time that we get ready to celebrate Jesus' birthday. Then, ask the children to tell what their family does to prepare for Christmas. (Opens an Advent calendar; decorates a tree; bakes cookies; makes gifts.)

### LISTENING

Collect the church newsletter, the Sunday bulletin, flyers, or any other information that tells of upcoming Advent activities in your church.

**Begin by asking the children if some of the Christmas preparations and activities that they do at home with their families are also done at church by the church family. (Decorating a tree; helping a needy family; setting up créche scenes.)**
**Next, ask them to think of ways the church celebrates that is different than at home. (Special music programs; caroling in nursing homes; Christmas pageants.) Then bring out your church Advent information and share with the children all that is going on in your church. Follow up with these questions: "What special things are we doing in worship to prepare for Jesus' birthday? (Lighting Advent candles; singing carols.) Are we having Advent activities for families and kids? (A caroling party; decorating workday; Christmas party.) Is our church showing Christlike love in our community by helping others? (Collecting food; helping a family; visiting shut-ins.) Are we celebrating Jesus' birthday by decorating?" (Wreaths; trees; candles; banners.)**
**Conclude by saying, "At church, we prepare for Jesus' birth by worshiping God, by enjoying activities as a church family, by helping others, and by showing our happiness with decorations."**

### EXPLORING

Assemble with the children an Advent counting activity to take home. For each child you'll need: one copy of the "Jesus' Birthday Candles" reproducible, one luncheon size paper bag, a seventy-two-inch length of red or green yarn, and crayons. Before Children's Church cut each reproducible candle sheet into individual squares. Punch a hole on the flame end of each candle.

Hand out the bags and ask the children to decorate them with a Christmas picture. While the group is coloring, explain that everyone will get a lot of paper candles to put in the bag along with a piece of yarn. When they get home, their parents can help them hang the yarn. Each day they are to pull a candle out of the bag, color it, and string it on the yarn. When the string is full and the bag is empty, it's time for Christmas! When the bags are decorated, place a piece of yarn and the candles in each bag.

When parents arrive to pick up their children, explain the Advent counting activity to them, too. Children should begin stringing candles on the yarn on December 1.

### SNACKING
It's especially fun to taste the first Christmas cookie of the season! Bake or purchase cookies for your group, or consider bringing in ready-made cookie dough and decorations and letting the children decorate the cookies themselves. Preheat the oven and bake the cookies in your church kitchen.

### MORE EXPLORING
Sing Christmas carols or listen to Christmas carols on tape. Children like to sing their favorites over and over again. They can take turns ringing the bell from the Children's Church Kit as a festive addition to the joyful noise.

### MORE SONGS from *Sing a New Song*
An Angel Told Mary, 35
Joseph, the Carpenter, 22
Let Us Go to Nazareth, 21

*Counting the Days of Advent*

# Christmas

*"But the angel said to them, 'Do not be afraid; for see—I am bringing you good news of great joy for all the people.' "*
*Luke 2:10*

### MESSAGE
Angels told the good news of Jesus' birth to shepherds.

### OPENING
Music and Movement: Christmas Is Such a Happy Time, page 35, *Sing a New Song*

Following Music and Movement, ask the children to sit in a circle.

### SHARING
Begin by asking the children to tell of a time when they were told good news. (We won a prize; my baby brother was born; Daddy said he could fix my toy.) Continue by asking, "How did this good news make you feel?" (Happy; excited.) Explain that today's story is about shepherds who hear some very good news.

### LISTENING
Before Children's Church, prepare "The Shepherd's Story Strip" reproducible; one copy per child. Cut each sheet into three strips along indicated lines and tape the three strips together so the pictures are sequential.

Just before you read the story, give the children story strips to look at as they listen. Read Luke 2:7-20 directly from the Bible.

### PRAYING
Tell the children to put their story strips on the floor and stand for the prayer. Ask all to raise their hands high in the air and wiggle their fingers when you say the words "We praise you":

**God in the highest; we praise you!**

**You make wonderful things happen; we praise you!**

**You sent Jesus to us as a little baby; we praise you!**

**We celebrate because it is Jesus' birthday; we praise you! Amen.**

### EXPLORING
The Shepherd's Story Strip will become a take-home Christmas ornament. You'll need crayons, a hole punch, and yarn cut into twelve-inch lengths to turn the strips into an accordion-pleated booklet.

Have the children color the strip. When the coloring is finished, pleat the strip by folding the line between picture one and two, making sure that picture one faces outward. The fold between pictures two and three will make the pictures face each other. Repeat the outward-inward folding until the strip is completely folded. After you demonstrate, the children may be able to do the folding, or you may need to do it for them.

To finish, compress the folded strip between your fingers with the title page facing you. Punch two holes on the left-hand folded side. Thread a length of yarn and knot with a bow or a loop.

### SNACKING
Treat the children with candy canes! Explain that candy canes are shaped like a shepherd's staff and were created in honor of the Christmas shepherds.

### MORE EXPLORING
Lead this Shepherd's Story song, asking the children to join in the singing and the actions. The song is sung to the tune of "Mary Had a Little Lamb":

The shepherds had a flock of sheep, flock of sheep, flock of sheep,

The shepherds had a flock of sheep they cared for night and day (look around with hand sheltering eyes).

Everywhere the flock went, flock went, flock went,

Everywhere the flock went, the shepherds had to go (walk in place).

One night an angel came to them, came to them, came to them,

One night an angel came to them, which scared the shepherds so (hold palms to the sides of face).

The angel said to find the child, find the child, find the child,

The angel said to find the child, in a manger bed (clasp own hands together and rock arms side to side).

The shepherds found the Savior child, Savior child, Savior child,
The shepherds found the Savior child, then they praised the Lord (raise arms up and wiggle fingers).

**OTHER SONGS** from *Sing a New Song*
Away in a Manger, 37
Come Softly, Walk Gently, 38
Shepherd, Shepherd, 41

---

# Epiphany

*"Wise men from the East came to Jerusalem, asking, 'Where is the child who has been born king of the Jews?'"*
*Matthew 2:1-2*

### MESSAGE
Wise men saw a sign from God and came to honor the baby Jesus.

### OPENING
Music and Movement: I'd Like to Ride a Camel, page 42, *Sing a New Song*
Following Music and Movement, ask the children to sit in a circle.

### SHARING
Give the children an opportunity to tell the group about a favorite gift they have received. (This does not have to be a Christmas gift.) After everyone responds, say that the best gift God has sent the world is his son, Jesus. When Jesus was born, wise men came to honor him with gifts of their own.

### LISTENING
With the sheet from the Children's Church Kit draped over your head and shoulders, give a first person account of the wise men's journey:

Greetings to you, followers of Jesus! I am one of the wise men who followed a special star and found the baby Jesus. Open your ears and hear my story.

We were studying the stars and how they move in the night sky. One evening we saw an unusual star and we knew that it was a sign from God. We began our journey right away. We followed the star to the city of Jerusalem where King Herod ruled the Roman Empire. We asked the people in the city where we could find the child who was born King of the Jews. We told them that we were following his very special star and we wished we could visit him and honor him.

My stars! Our questions seemed to get the whole city in an uproar. Everyone wondered who this child king was and where he was living. Old King Herod was especially curious. He called in all the Jewish church leaders and they explained that a Messiah would be born in Bethlehem of Judea.

In the twinkling of an eye, King Herod had a secret meeting with us. He was afraid of this baby born to be king. He enjoyed being king and didn't want anyone to take his place. He asked us many questions, then told us to go find the child. King Herod said we should come back to tell him where the child king was living, so he could visit him too.

Quicker than the wink of a camel's eye, we set off to Bethlehem. We were filled with great joy when the star we had followed for so many days finally stopped moving! We went into the house and found the child with his mother, Mary. We got down on our tired knees to worship and honor the child. We each gave Jesus a gift. I gave him gold. My friends gave him sweet smelling frankincense and the valuable medicine, myrrh.

After our visit with Mary and Jesus, I was filled with happiness until I had a strange dream. In my dream God warned me that I should not go back to see Herod. We left Bethlehem by a different way to keep from meeting Herod again.

I believe that God in heaven has sent the world a precious gift, this child, Jesus. I am thankful that I could see the Messiah. Please excuse me (yawn) I have been up all night watching the stars. I'm so sleepy.

### PRAYING

Have children stand with their feet apart and hands held out from their sides. They are stars! Ask them to close their eyes for this prayer:

Dear God,
  Thanks for the wise men who traveled so far, and thanks to you for sending the star! Amen.

### EXPLORING

The children will enjoy making modeling dough stars. Here are four star-making techniques:

Cut star shapes out of index cards to use as a pattern over flattened modeling dough. Cut dough with plastic knives.

To make rolled stars, start with five 1-inch balls of dough. Roll each into a short log and make a star shape by joining the tips of each log together at one center.

Pinch a star from a flat circle of dough by making five pinches around the edge of the circle.

To make stars from triangles, use a plastic knife to cut two triangles from flattened dough. Lay them one over the other, so that the six points form a star.

After cleaning up the dough stars, present the children with foil stars on the backs of their hands.

### SNACKING

Make the snack into a gift by covering it in gift wrap and ribbon. Children delight in individual gifts to unwrap, but if you have a large group, the snack may be placed in a box and wrapped. Also remember that after-Christmas sales are a great source of fancy-wrapped treats at reasonable prices.

### MORE EXPLORING

To celebrate Epiphany, play Star Search. Cut six stars each from five different color sheets of construction paper. Before Children's Church, hide the stars about the room.

To play, divide the group into five teams. Ask each team to search for stars of a certain color. If time permits, each team can hide the stars they found, then each team can be assigned a new color for which to search.

**OTHER SONGS** from *Sing a New Song*
Mary Had a Baby, 40
The New Little Baby Boy, 41
The Church Has Many Colors, 34

*Modeling Dough Star*

# Palm Sunday

*"A very large crowd spread
their cloaks on the road, and
others cut branches from the trees
and spread them on the road."*
Matthew 21:8

## MESSAGE
People believed in Jesus and honored him.

## OPENING
Music and Movement: Hosanna, page 45, *Sing a New Song*

Following Music and Movement, ask the children to sit in a circle.

## SHARING
Invite each child to tell if he or she has seen a parade or been in one. Then explain to the children that nowadays we see parades on TV or in our towns. However, in Jesus' day, parades were special and did not happen very often.

## LISTENING
Share the story of Jesus' triumphant entry into Jerusalem from Matthew 21:1-11:

Many, many years before Jesus was born, prophets said that God's people would see their king coming to them as a gentle man seated on a donkey. It happened just as the prophets said it would.

Jesus and his followers were walking to Jerusalem. When they came to the Mount of Olives, Jesus asked two of his followers to go to a nearby village and find a donkey and her baby colt and bring them back to him. Jesus walked everywhere he wanted to go. In fact, almost everyone walked. Only a few people rode horses. The people who owned donkeys used them for their work.

The followers found a donkey and her colt. They brought them to Jesus and covered them with their cloaks. Jesus sat on the animals. Then, Jesus and his followers went to Jerusalem.

A large crowd gathered along the road to see Jesus. Many people took off their robes and cloaks and spread them on the road to show Jesus their love and respect. Other believers cut palm branches from trees and placed the fresh green leaves on the road. All the people cheered "Hosanna in the highest heaven" and "Blessed is the one who comes in the name of the Lord!" as Jesus passed.

As the excited and happy crowd came into Jerusalem with Jesus, the whole city became stirred with excitement and wonder. Some city people asked, "Who is this man?" The crowds said, "This is Jesus from Nazareth of Galilee."

This was the parade for Jesus. There were cloaks and branches spread on the road; there were joyous crowds of believers; there was praise and love and honor showered on Jesus as he rode into the city. This was an important day for Jesus and an important day for God's people, as they saw God's son, a gentle king, coming to them on a donkey.

## PRAYING
Explain to the children that in the language of Jesus, the word "Hosanna" meant "praise God" or "praise Jesus." Ask them to shout Hosanna with you three times. Next, ask them to close their eyes and bow their heads as you shout Hosanna three times together to praise God in a prayer. Conclude the prayer by saying "Amen."

## EXPLORING
Make easy palm branches from nine-by-twelve-inch construction paper to wave in a pretend parade for Jesus.

For every nine children, you'll need 1 piece of brown construction paper, 4½ pieces of green construction paper, and 9 brad fasteners. You'll also need a ruler, pencil, scissors, and hole punch to prepare the paper for this activity.

To make branch handles, take one sheet of brown paper and measure nine one-inch marks across the nine-inch end of the paper. Using the marks as a guide, cut nine one-by-twelve-inch strips. Fold each strip in half, then punch through the folded strip, ½-inch from the unfolded end.

Next, make palm leaves from the green paper. Cut the paper across the width to give nine pieces measuring six-by-nine-inches. Measure nine one-inch marks along the nine-inch side of each sheet and cut into strips one-by-six-inches. In one end of each strip, punch a hole ½-inch from the end. To finish the palm leaves, snip the corners of the end that isn't punched, so the leaves will be pointed. You will have nine palm leaves per branch handle.

To assemble, instruct the children to point the brad through one hole of the brown branch handle; put on all of the leaves, then put the brad through the other hole in the branch handle. (If you are concerned that young children may put the brads in their mouths, staple the leaves instead.) After they open the wings of the brad, the children can fold and unfold their palm branches to pretend to wave in a parade for Jesus.

### SNACKING

Use a paring knife to cut long slits in stalks of celery to create pretend palm branches. Start at the wide end, cutting two-thirds of the way down the stalk. Try to make 3 or 4 slits to form the palm leaves. Finish with a touch of peanut butter on the uncut end to make it look like a real branch.

### MORE EXPLORING

Create a bright "Hosanna" banner by drawing large block letters on a nine-foot length of shelf or craft paper. Spread the paper on a table with crayons and let the children use their imaginations to decorate the letters.

**OTHER SONGS** from *Sing a New Song*
Jesus Is Riding, 43
When Jesus Came to Jerusalem, 44
Happy All the Time, 94

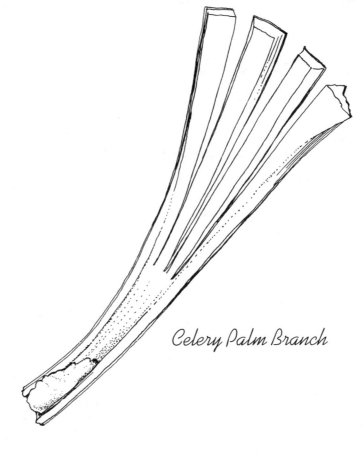

*Celery Palm Branch*

# Easter

*"As she wept, she bent over to look into the tomb; and she saw two angels in white, sitting where the body of Jesus had been lying."*
*John 20:11-12*

## MESSAGE

After dying on the cross, Jesus was brought back to life by God.

## OPENING

Music and Movement: "Alleluia," Children Sing, page 45, *Sing a New Song*

Following Music and Movement, ask the children to sit in a circle.

## SHARING

Ask the children to share what Easter means to them. (Candy from the Easter Bunny; egg hunts; a new dress; Jesus dying and coming to life again.)

## LISTENING

Begin by explaining:

**Colored eggs, baskets of candy, and new clothes are things we do to celebrate God's promise of new life. Jesus, God's son, died on a cross. Three days after he died, God brought Jesus back to life. This showed people that God can give us new life after we die.**

Read the Resurrection Story directly from the Bible, John 20:1-16. You will review the story with the children during "Exploring."

## PRAYING

Ask the children to bow their heads and close their eyes as you pray:

**Dear God, Today we are celebrating your promise of new life after death. We thank you for sending Jesus to the world to help us and teach us. We believe in Jesus and in life after death. Amen.**

## EXPLORING

Children will "roll away the stone" to better understand the story.

For each child, you'll need a paper plate, one brad fastener, a five-inch circle of construction paper, and crayons. Before Children's Church, trace a five-inch circle onto the center of each plate. This is the "tomb." Next, trace and cut an equal number of five-inch circles from construction paper. These are the "stones." Affix the construction-paper stone over the center of the tomb with a brad fastener punched through the plate near the edge of the stone. (If you are concerned that young children may put the brads in their mouths, staple the stone to the plate.) The stone can be pivoted away to reveal the tomb in the center of the plate.

To begin the activity, give each child a plate you have crafted. Explain that the paper circle on the plate is a pretend stone. Invite the children to color the stone to make it look more interesting. As they color, ask the children if they remember a stone as part of the Bible story. (Mary saw that the stone was removed from the tomb.) Tell everyone that a very big stone was put over the opening of Jesus' tomb to keep animals or people from bothering his body. It was very hard to move the stone, and when Mary saw it pushed back from the opening, she was worried.

Next, tell the children to roll away the stone on their plate tomb. Ask them what the disciples saw inside the tomb. (They saw wrappings from Jesus' body.) Remind the children that the disciples went home and Mary stayed at the tomb, crying. Ask the children what Mary saw when she bent over to look into the tomb. (Two angels.) Tell the children to draw two angels in the center of the plate (inside the tomb). While the children color, tell them that Mary first saw the angels, then she saw a man. When he called her name, she knew that it was Jesus. He had risen from the dead!

When the children have finished drawing their angels, ask them to cover the opening to the tomb with the paper stone. Ask: "Is Jesus in the tomb?" (No.) Continue: "Now roll away the stone." (Pause.) Ask: "Who is in the tomb?" (Angels.) If time permits, tell children that the tomb was in a garden and that they may decorate the rest of the plate with flowers and grasses.

### SNACKING

Serve candy eggs or real hard-boiled eggs. Explain to children that eggs are a symbol of a new life, the life we have with Jesus.

### MORE EXPLORING

Use the ball from the Children's Church Kit to play an Easter Ball Game. Have the children sit or stand in a circle. Begin by saying, "(Child's name) roll away the stone!" and then roll the ball to that child. The child with the ball will call another child's name and say, "roll away the stone," then roll the ball to that child. Encourage the child with the ball to call on someone who hasn't had a turn, until all have had a chance to roll the ball.

### OTHER SONGS from Sing a New Song

Do Lord, 55
Down in My Heart, 54
There's Music All Inside Me, 88

---

# Pentecost

## "All who believed were together."
### Acts 2:44

### MESSAGE

God sent the Holy Spirit to help the disciples on Pentecost and this was the beginning of the church.

### OPENING

Music and Movement: A Helper I Will Be, page 83, Sing a New Song

Following Music and Movement, ask the children to sit in a circle.

### SHARING

Pose this question to the children, "Who helps you when you need help?" (Parents; teachers or caregivers; friends; God.)

### LISTENING

Tell a simplified version of the Pentecost story from Acts 2:1-47:

**God can send us help in many ways. God can give us a person to help us, such as a teacher or a friend; God can help us through our church family; and God can help us through the Holy Spirit. In this Bible story, God sends the Holy Spirit to help the disciples. With the help of the Holy Spirit, the disciples begin the Christian Church.**

**This story takes place after Jesus died. God had brought Jesus back to life and the disciples had seen him and talked with him. Then Jesus went up into heaven.**

**The disciples had come together for a holy day called "Pentecost." All of a sudden a sound like a mighty wind filled the house, and tongues that looked like fire touched each disciple. Then the disciples began to talk in different languages. The Holy Spirit had come to them. The Holy Spirit was a helper sent by God.**

**There were visitors from other countries in the city because of this holy day. These visitors spoke many different languages. When the visitors in the street heard the great noise at the house, they gathered to see what was happening. Much to the people's surprise, the disciples spoke to the crowd. They spoke in the languages that the visitors spoke and understood. Everyone heard about Jesus and the wonderful things that God had done.**

Then Peter, one of the disciples, talked to the crowd, explaining that Jesus was the Messiah and that he had been raised from the dead by God. Peter told everyone that if they believed in Jesus, they would be saved from their sins and have new life after death.

The Holy Spirit helped Peter and the other disciples to speak in other languages so that people from other countries could understand the news about Jesus. These new believers joined together to pray, to talk, and to eat together. This is how the Christian Church began.

### PRAYING

Ask the children to repeat the words and movements after you:

**We praise you God in highest heaven** (raise arms straight up with fingers pointing upward).

**We believe in Jesus Christ** (stretch arms out in front to form a cross).

**We thank you for the Holy Spirit** (wave arms at sides, like wings),

**And for churches that believers have begun** (raise arms over head, touching fingertips together to form a steeple).

**Amen** (hands folded, heads bowed).

### EXPLORING

Combine the symbols for the church and the mighty wind from Pentecost to create a Pentecost Fan Pendant.

Give each child a four-by-six-inch index card to decorate before folding into a fan. The children may decorate the card with a crayon drawing of their church or glue on pictures of the church that you have pre-cut from old bulletins or newsletters.

After the cards are decorated, show the children how to fold the cards with an accordion pleat. Six folds, about one-inch wide across the width of the card makes for a good fan shape.

To assemble the fan pendant, you'll need a stapler and a forty-two-inch length of yarn. Pinch the fan together at one end and staple. Then staple the two ends of the yarn to the pinched end, leaving a six-inch tail on each end below the staple. Finish by tying the ends into a bow. The children can wear their fans around their necks to remember Pentecost.

### SNACKING

Pentecost is often called "The Birthday of the Church." Celebrate with a cake or cupcakes. For additional fun, use birthday candles and sing "Happy Birthday."

### MORE EXPLORING

Bring out all of the items in the Children's Church Kit and challenge the children to think of ways that the items could be used to help begin a new church. For example, the rock could be used in the building; the doll could be the first baby baptized; the toy animal could be a toy for the nursery; the container of pennies could help buy things for the church; the blanket could be used to cover the altar; the bell could be a church bell; the ball could be a toy for bigger kids; and the basket could hold the offering.

**MORE SONGS** from *Sing a New Song*
Praise the Lord, 49
The Church Has Many Colors, 34
We Are Messengers, 32

Cut apart on dotted lines and punch a hole in each flame for hanging.

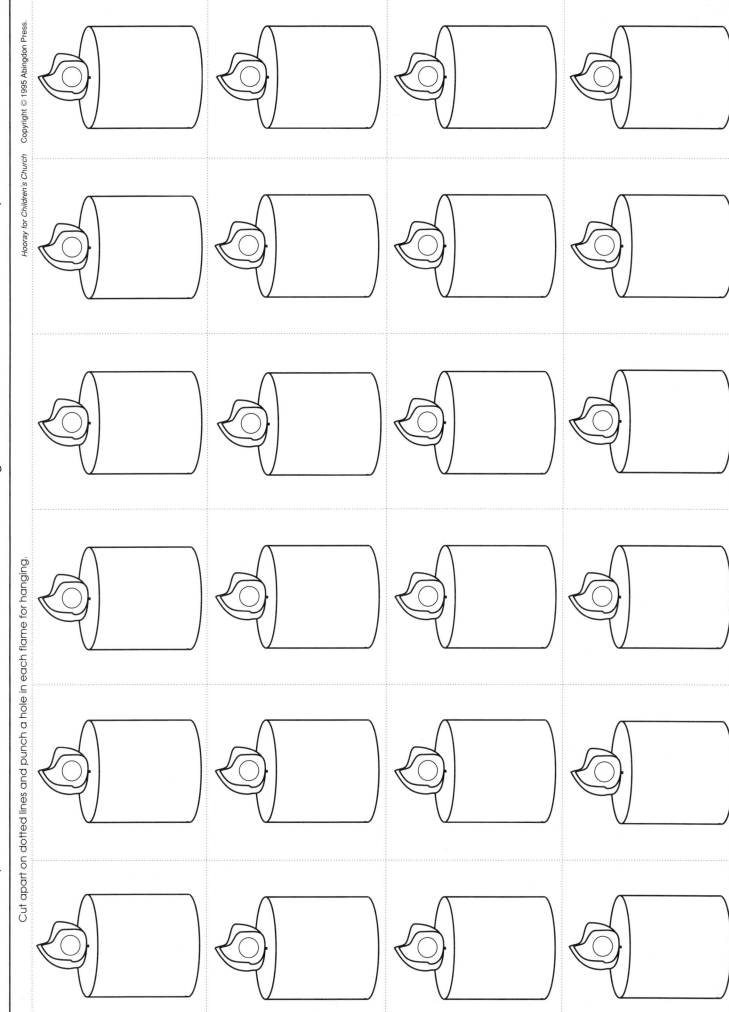

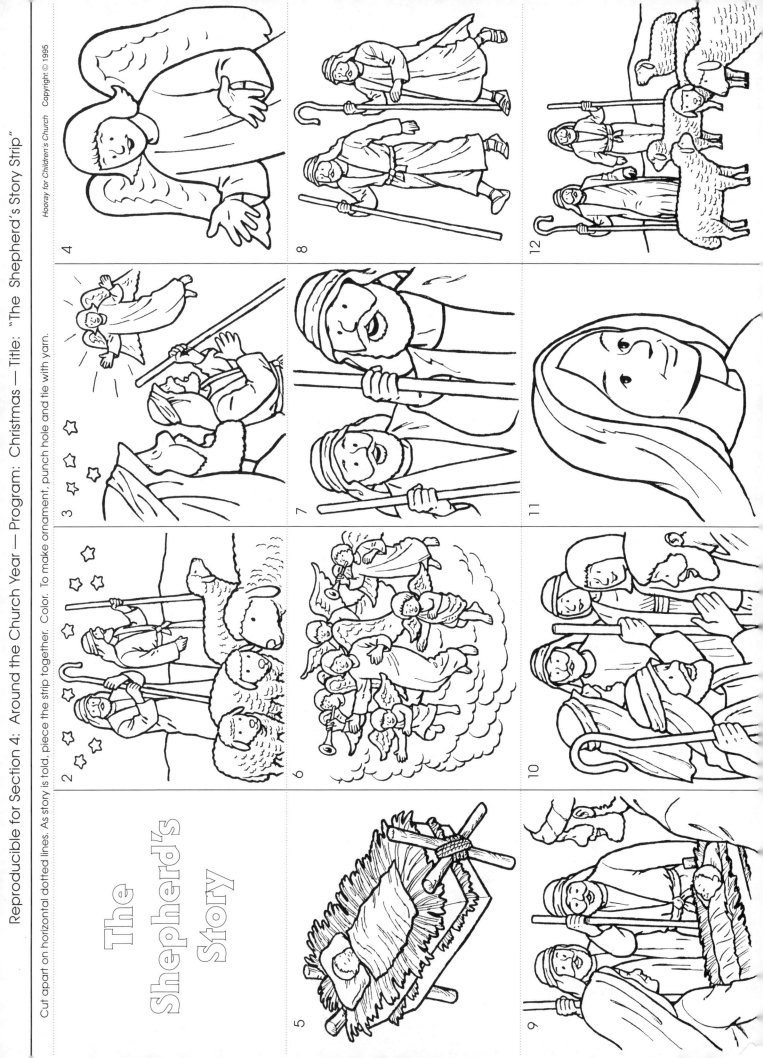

Reproducible for Section 4: Around the Church Year — Program: Christmas — Title: "The Shepherd's Story Strip"

Cut apart on horizontal dotted lines. As story is told, piece the strip together. Color. To make ornament, punch hole and tie with yarn.

Hooray for Children's Church   Copyright © 1995

The
Shepherd's
Story

2
3
4
5
6
7
8
9
10
11
12

## God Created Families

*"God blessed them, and God said to them, 'Be fruitful and multiply.' "*
*Genesis 1:28*

### OPENING

Music and Movement: In Our Family, page 80, *Sing a New Song*

Following Music and Movement, ask the children to sit in a circle.

### MESSAGE

God created families.

### LISTENING

To introduce the story, use a brown paper luncheon size bag as a Surprise Bag. Tuck a paper family inside. Cut out pictures of people from magazines or cut simple figures from paper and add features and clothing. Include a mother and father, a baby, and several older siblings. Put the figures inside the bag and don't let the children peek inside. Begin:

**I brought a Surprise Bag with me today. Let's open it and see what's inside. (One by one, bring out the figures and introduce them.) This is the mother; this is the father; this is the baby; this is the brother. . . . (Hold up all the paper people.) Together, what do these people make? (A family.)**

**God created families. God made families to live together, to take care of one another, to help one another, and to have fun with each other. Not every family is just like the one I showed you. Some children don't have brothers or sisters. Sometimes children live with just their mother or** their father, or perhaps they live with a grandparent, an aunt, or a foster parent. The people you live with are your family.

### SHARING

Ask the children to tell one activity that their family enjoys doing together. (We like to work in the garden; my family likes going out for ice cream; we have fun when we go on hikes in the woods.)

### PRAYING

Have children practice this motion prayer with you, then say it together:

**Families work (pretend to sweep the floor), And families play (pretend to throw a ball), Families love each other day by day (cross arms on chest and turn body from side to side). Thank you, God, for families (jump in air with arms held high). Amen.**

### EXPLORING

Children will create family portraits. Make frames for the portraits by folding construction paper in half and cutting about a one-inch border. Each frame will be glued to a sheet of white paper. You may do the gluing ahead of time or with the children.

Explain that a family portrait is a drawing or painting of a family. Museums have portraits of families that are hundreds of years old. Many family portraits include family pets. Ask the children to close their eyes and picture their families. Next, pass out the paper and the crayons and have the children create their family portraits.

When the portraits are finished, glue the frames on if you didn't do this ahead of time. If time permits, ask each child to show his or her portrait and tell the names of the family members. Hang the pictures somewhere in the church for all to see or send them home with the children.

### SNACKING

Tell the children that even though they certainly aren't babies anymore, you thought that it would be fun to serve a food that their parents served them as babies. Give each child a bowl of applesauce and a teething biscuit or plain cookie.

### MORE EXPLORING

Set out modeling dough and let the children have fun creating families.

### MORE SONGS from *Sing a New Song*

Thank You, God, for Loving Me, 81
Thankful Am I, 79
The Family of God, 80

# Honor Your Father and Mother

*"Honor your father and your mother."*
*Exodus 20:12*

### MESSAGE

God wants us to honor our parents.

### OPENING

Music and Movement: In Our Family, page 80, *Sing a New Song*
Following Music and Movement, ask the children to sit in a circle.

### SHARING

Ask the children to each say something they especially like about either their mother or their father. (My dad likes to play chase with me; my mom reads me stories; my dad makes me pancakes.) If children in your group live with someone other than their parents, such as a grandparent or foster parent, explain that those who love them and take care of them do the job of a parent.

### PRAYING

Ask the children to close their eyes as you guide them through this visualization prayer. Begin:

**Make a picture in your mind of your parents. Picture their hair, their eyes, their smiles (pause). Picture doing something special with them such as playing a game or going on a picnic (pause). Now picture something special that they do for you such as tying your shoes or fixing your breakfast (pause). Keep your eyes closed while we pray:**
**Thank you God for our parents and all they do for us. Amen.**

### LISTENING

During the story, children will give the "thumbs up" and the "thumbs down" signal in response to various situations:

**We've talked about what makes our parents special to us. The Bible says, "Honor your father and your mother." Because our parents love us and help us, God wants us to be kind to them, listen to them, and thank them for all they do. This is how we honor our parents.**

Let's play the Thumbs Up, Thumbs Down Game. I'm going to read you a situation. Use your thumbs up to tell me when a child is honoring his or her parents and thumbs down to tell when a child is being disrespectful and not honoring his or her parents. Let's begin:

When his mother told him to pick up his toys, Daniel said, "No way!" (Thumbs down.)

Sam gave his father a big hug. (Thumbs up.)

Antonio drew his mother a picture. (Thumbs up.)

Sandy was so angry she kicked her father. (Thumbs down.)

Marcos helped his mother by rocking his baby brother. (Thumbs up.)

Latoya refused to eat her mashed potatoes and dumped them on the kitchen floor. (Thumbs down.)

When her mother said, "Bedtime," Maggie put her hands over her ears and shouted, "Shut up!" (Thumbs down.)

Erin said, "Mom, you're great!" (Thumbs up.)

All the kids in Children's Church made Medals of Honor to give to their parents. (Thumbs up.)

## EXPLORING

Children will make Medals of Honor with paper, crayons, foil stars, and string to present to their parents. Use an object about six inches in diameter to trace circles onto light-colored construction paper. You will need two medals for each child. Punch a hole about one inch from the edge of each medal. Cut lengths of string about forty inches long. You may string and knot the medals ahead of time or help the children string and knot them after they have finished decorating.

Tell the children: "A Medal of Honor is a prize given to someone for something special that they have done. Your parents do lots of special things for you. Today you're going to make Medals of Honor to present to them."

Pass out the crayons and foil stars. Children may make a medal for each parent. Children who live with only one parent may make their second medal for someone else who is special to them. The medals, designed to be worn around the neck, can be presented to the parents when they arrive to pick up their children.

## SNACKING

In England in centuries past, Mothering Sunday, a forerunner to our Mother's Day, was celebrated on the Fourth Sunday in Lent. Children would return home to visit their mothers, bringing a gift of cake or bread. Explain this old custom to the children as you serve them cake, snack cakes, or a simple sweet bread.

## MORE EXPLORING

The children can play charades by acting out some of the things their parents do for them: fixing meals, tying shoes, teaching them to say their prayers, reading a story, or giving a hug. If children have trouble thinking of ideas, you can whisper suggestions to them. If you have reluctant actors, you can act out the charade or have the child act it out along with you.

**MORE SONGS** from *Sing a New Song*
Thank You, God, for Loving Me, 81
The Family of God, 80
Thankful Am I, 79

# Parents Protect Us

*"Then Joseph got up, took the child and his mother by night, and went to Egypt."*
Matthew 2:14

### MESSAGE
God wants parents to protect their children.

### OPENING
Music and Movement: Children Everywhere, page 78, *Sing a New Song*

Following Music and Movement, ask the children to sit in a circle.

### LISTENING
The story is told through the eyes of Joseph:

**Hello. My name is Joseph. I am the father of Jesus. God is Jesus' heavenly father but he has chosen me to be the father of Jesus on earth. Let me tell you something scary that happened to us. After Jesus was born, I had a dream. An angel appeared in my dream and said, "Take the child and his mother and flee to Egypt and stay there until I tell you. King Herod is looking for the child and plans to kill him." I took Mary and Jesus to Egypt, which is far away from where we live. I wanted to protect my son.**

**After a while, I had another dream. This dream told me that King Herod had died and that we could go back to our homeland. I'm glad that I was able to protect Jesus from the evil king who wanted to kill him.**

### SHARING
Ask the children to each tell about a time when their parents protected them. (My dad pulled me out of the pool when I fell in the deep end; my mother caught me when I was falling from the monkey bars; my mom makes sure I wear my seat belt in case we have an accident.)

### PRAYING
Ask the children to huddle together for a Huddle Prayer. When all are settled, have them close their eyes while you pray:

**Dear God, We're glad that Joseph protected his son, Jesus. Thank you for giving us parents who protect us. Amen.**

### EXPLORING
Children will make hand puppets from the "Mary and Baby Jesus" reproducible. Make copies of the puppet, then staple a sheet of white paper underneath each puppet. Make sure the staples are inside the cutting lines.

Explain to the children that Mary, Jesus' mother, protected her baby, too. Hand out the reproducible and ask the children to color the puppet. After the puppet has been colored, have the children cut it out. Although the cutting is fairly simple, you may need to assist those who don't have much experience with scissors.

### SNACKING
Mary and Joseph had to eat on the road while they were fleeing to Egypt. Prepare a snack for a journey such as peanut butter and jelly sandwiches or crackers and cheese. You may want to add some water or juice in a jug, and paper cups. Place the snack in a knapsack and take the children on a short journey to eat the snack. If it isn't practical to eat in another location, they will still enjoy the excitement of watching their snack unpacked from a knapsack.

### MORE EXPLORING
Play the game, Fleeing to Egypt. Seat the children in a circle and ask, "What would you take if you were told to flee to Egypt?" Children answer by saying, "I'm fleeing to Egypt and I'm taking (*fill-in*)." (My teddy bear.) The next child says what the first person is taking and adds something: "I'm fleeing to Egypt and I'm taking my teddy bear and my blanket." The game continues around the circle. If children have trouble remembering as the list gets long, the whole group can say it together.

**MORE SONGS** from *Sing a New Song*
Jesus Loves Me, 29
Joseph, the Carpenter, 22
Thank You, God, for Loving Me, 81

# Obey Your Parents

*"Children, obey your parents*
*in the Lord, for this is right."*
Ephesians 6:1

## MESSAGE
God expects children to obey their parents.

## OPENING
Music and Movement: God Gifted Me, page 78, *Sing a New Song*

Following Music and Movement, ask the children to sit in a circle.

## SHARING
Ask the children to tell about a time when they disobeyed their parents. (My mother told me to stay in the yard but I went into the street; My dad said, "Just one cookie" but I took three; I'm not allowed to hit my sister but I did.)

## LISTENING
Talk to the children about obeying their parents:

**It isn't always easy for children to obey their parents. Sometimes it's difficult isn't it? God has given you parents to take care of you. Good parents are grown-ups who want to keep you safe and teach you how to behave. Your parents love you and they want what is best for you, even though it may not always seem that way. By obeying our parents, we are obeying God too.**

**The word "obey" comes from a French word that means "to hear" or "to listen." When you listen carefully to what your parents say to you, then you will have an easier time obeying them.**

## PRAYING
Ask the children to close their eyes and bow their heads as you pray:

**Dear God, It isn't always easy to obey our parents but we know that this is what you want us to do. Help us to be good listeners. Amen.**

## EXPLORING
To help them think about listening carefully, let the children play an old-fashioned game of Mother, or Father, May I? Line the children up at one end of the room. Explain that they may only move if they ask Mother (or Father, if you're a man) May I? Give simple, yet creative commands such as "Jason, you may take one frog leap forward" or "Courtney, you may take ten baby steps forward." If a child asks "Mother May I?" then he or she may move forward. If a child moves without asking permission, than he or she may not go forward.

As children reach you, ask them to sit down and watch the others finish the game. Instead of declaring a winner, the game is finished when all of the children have successfully reached you. Other commands might include: twirl, hop on one foot, tiptoe, gallop, crab walk, bunny hop, take a giant step, and take a gliding step. You may want to demonstrate the steps ahead of time.

## SNACKING
One of the ways that children are asked to obey is to use correct table manners. Set a "fancy" table for the snack, using real dishes, tea cups, and silverware, if your church has them. A tablecloth, pretty paper napkins, and even a centerpiece add to the fun. Offer fruit salad in a bowl (so children may practice serving themselves), a plate of cookies, and cups of juice. Remind the children to eat with their best company manners, just as their parents ask them to do when they have dinner guests at home.

## MORE EXPLORING
Children love to play pretend "parents and children." Divide the group into pairs. One child is to be the parent, the other the child. They may decide this themselves, or you can assign the roles if it's simpler for you to do so. If time permits, they can play again, switching roles. Guide them through an imaginary trip to the grocery store. If the children don't quite catch on, give them some of the hints in parentheses.

"Parents, we're on the way to the grocery store. Show your children how you want them to sit in the car and tell them how to behave." (Buckle seat belts; no shouting or screaming; don't throw things out the window.)

"Parents, drive to the store." (Parents pretend to drive; children can pretend to either obey or disobey.)

"Parents, here we are. Help your children get into the store safely." (Hold hands; don't jump in the mud puddle.)

"We're in the store now. Parents, tell your children how you expect them to behave, then begin your shopping." (No begging for treats; no running; stay with parent; no standing up in the cart; don't touch breakable items such as the jars of pickles; don't squeeze the bread.)

"Parents, you're in the checkout line." (Say hello to the checker; don't climb on the counter; don't beg for candy; say good-bye to the checker.)

"Parents, let's load up the groceries and drive home." (Don't beg to open cookies; stay by the car and get in when asked to.)

"Now we're home." (Children can help carry in lightweight groceries; help put groceries away; maybe they could have just one cookie!)

**MORE SONGS** from *Sing a New Song*
A Helper I Will Be, 83
Love One Another, 82
Abraham's Family, 58

---

# Families Forgive

*"But while he was still far off, his father saw him and was filled with compassion."*
*Luke 15:20*

### MESSAGE
Family members forgive one another.

### OPENING
Music and Movement: Forgiveness, page 33, *Sing a New Song*
Following Music and Movement, ask the children to sit in a circle.

### LISTENING
Retell the parable of the prodigal son (Luke 15:11-32). Explain to the children that "prodigal" means to waste money or to spend too much money:

**This is a story that Jesus told about forgiveness. It is called the story of the prodigal son.**

**Once there was a man who had two sons. He gave each of his sons money. The younger son went to a distant country. He spent and wasted all of his money. He was hungry and decided to go home to his father. He decided that he would ask his father to forgive him for being a prodigal son. He was sorry that he left home and wasted all of the money his father gave him.**

**When the son was almost home, his father spotted him in the distance and announced, "My son is home. We're going to have a party to celebrate." The older son, who hadn't wasted his money, was angry. He said to his father, "I have stayed home and helped you but my brother left home and wasted all of his money. Why are you giving him a party?" The father replied, "I love you son, but I love your brother too. Your brother was lost but now he's found. I forgive him. We must be happy and have a party because he is home again."**

### SHARING
Tell the children, "The father in the story forgave his son because he loved him. Family members forgive one another." Ask the children to tell about a time when they forgave someone in their family. (My brother broke my new truck, but I forgave him;

66

my mom put me in my room and I forgave her; my father made me mad because he wouldn't take me for ice cream, but I forgave him.)

### PRAYING

Have the children form a prayer circle by placing their arms across one another's shoulders. Ask them to close their eyes and bow their heads as you pray:

**Forgiving God, Just as you forgive us and just as the father forgave his prodigal son, help us to forgive members of our family. Amen.**

### EXPLORING

Hand each child a copy of the "Welcome Home Maze" and pass out the crayons. Ask them to help the prodigal son find his way home through the maze. If time permits, they can then color the picture.

### SNACKING

Hold a Welcome Home Party for the prodigal son. Serve punch, perhaps from a real punch bowl, and cookies. Consider hanging balloons or streamers and even letting the children throw confetti!

### MORE EXPLORING

Using a length of shelf or craft paper, have the children make a welcome home banner for the prodigal son. Outline the letters "WELCOME HOME PRODIGAL SON!" and have the children color them in. When the banner is finished, lead them in singing this welcome home song to the tune of "For He's a Jolly Good Fellow":

**We're glad that you came home,**
**We're glad that you came home,**
**We're glad that you came home,**
**We forgive you for going away.**

**Come in, we'll have a party,**
**Come in, we'll have a party,**
**Come in, we'll have a party,**
**We're glad that you came home!**

**MORE SONGS** from *Sing a New Song*
Love One Another, 82
March, 87
The Family of God, 80

# Our Church Family

*"Let us work for the good of all,
and especially for those
of the family of faith."*
Galatians 6:10

### MESSAGE

Our church is a family of faith that helps one another.

### OPENING

Music and Movement: The Family of God, page 80, *Sing a New Song*

Following Music and Movement, ask the children to sit in a circle.

### LISTENING

Children will have fun responding to this story. Begin:

**You live in a family that takes care of you and helps you. Our church is like a family because we help one another. I'm going to tell you a story about a church family. When something bad happens you say, "Oh no!" When something good happens you say, "Oh yes!" I'll raise my hand when it's time for you to say "Oh no!" or "Oh yes!" (Practice the signal and the responses with the children.) Ready?**

**Lots was happening at the Green Valley Church. Mrs. Jones broke her leg (Oh No!), but people from church brought her dinners and raked her lawn (Oh yes!). Karen lost her ballet shoes the day before the dance recital (Oh no!), but a friend from church let Karen borrow hers (Oh yes!). Pastor Schultz locked his keys in his car (Oh no!), but Mr. Sanchez drove him home to pick up a spare set (Oh yes!). Jamie's mom and dad both had to work on the weekend (Oh no!), but Jamie was invited to stay at Natalie's house (Oh yes!). A new boy at church didn't know anyone and felt shy (Oh no!), but Tyler sat with him in Children's Church (Oh yes!). The furnace at the Chins' house broke down (Oh no!), but the Harpers said Mr. Chin and**

**his family could stay with them (Oh yes!). Mr. Califono was in the hospital (Oh no!), but the kids made him get well cards (Oh yes!). Often bad things happen to the people at Green Valley Church (Oh no!), but the church is a family and they help one another (Oh yes!).**

### SHARING

Ask the children to suggest ways that they can help people at church. (Help with the babies and toddlers; welcome newcomers; be friendly; make cards for sick members; invite kids from church to come over and play.)

### PRAYING

Before Children's Church, ask your pastor for the names of church members whom the congregation will be asked to remember in their prayers. Tell the children that one important way that the church family can help one another is through prayer. Explain that during the prayer you will say the names of individuals or families who need special prayers. If appropriate, also add the reason: Mrs. Hestler's mother, Jenny's grandma, died on Thursday; Mr. Rodriguez is in the hospital with pneumonia. Ask the children to bow their heads and close their eyes as you pray:

**God of our church family, We know that our church is a family of faith. We will try to help others at our church when they need our help. This morning we pray for these people (*fill in the names and their problem*). Help us to love one another just as you love us. Amen.**

### EXPLORING

The children will use four-by-six-inch index cards to make Hello Cards that can be sent to members of your church who would especially enjoy receiving them. Elderly members of a congregation love to receive cards from the church's children. The cards may be hand delivered (your pastor may appreciate a supply to keep on hand for visitation) or mailed. To mail, simply address the undecorated side of the card and attach a postcard stamp.

Explain to the children that they are going to make Hello Cards for members of their church family. They are to decorate only one side of the index card. Hand out the index cards and crayons. (Children will enjoy using colorful stickers too, if you have those available.) Write "HELLO" on paper or on the chalkboard for those who can write to copy. Those who know how can sign their names. If time permits, help the children who are unable to write. If time is short, later write "Hello from Children's Church" on the decorated cards before sending them.

### SNACKING

Prepare a food that your church family enjoys at potluck or covered dish suppers such as macaroni and cheese, deviled eggs, or gelatin salad. Explain to the children that church families enjoy sharing favorite foods together just as their family does.

### MORE EXPLORING

Before Children's Church, use a round object about six inches in diameter to trace circles onto a length of shelf or craft paper. Invite children to turn the circles into the faces of their church family. Label the mural "Our Church Family" and hang it up for all to admire.

**MORE SONGS** from *Sing a New Song*
Jesus' Hands Were Kind Hands, 26
The Things We Need, 92
Jesu, Jesu, 33

Staple art (½″ inside outline) to another piece of paper at sides and top. Leave bottom open to insert hand. Color.
Trim around outline cutting through both pieces of paper.

Help the prodigal son find his way home.

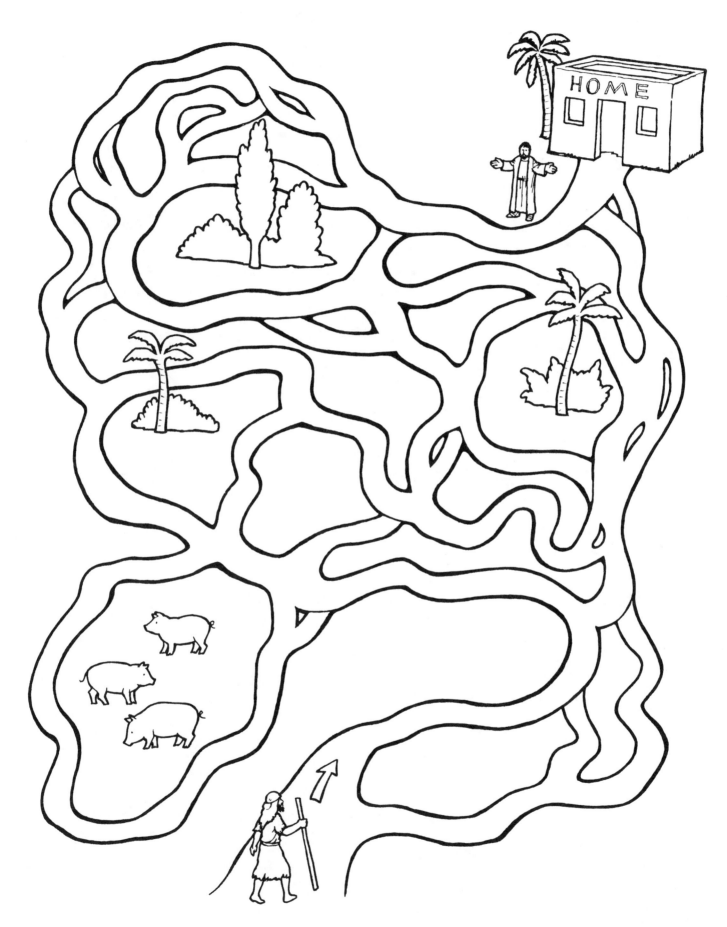

# THE LIFE OF JESUS

## Jesus Is Born

*"She gave birth to her firstborn son and wrapped him in bands of cloth, and laid him in a manger, because there was no place for them in the inn."*
Luke 2:7

### MESSAGE
God's son, Jesus, came into the world as a baby.

### OPENING
Music and Movement: The New Little Baby Boy, page 41, *Sing a New Song*

Following Music and Movement, ask the children to sit in a circle.

### PRAYING
Bring out the doll and the blanket from the Children's Church Kit. Wrap the doll in the blanket and cradle it in your arms. Tell the children that the "baby" will be passed around the circle.

As each child holds the baby, the group will say, **"Thank you, God, for babies and thank you for (child's name)."** Begin the prayer by handing the baby to a child and leading the litany. End the prayer by saying, **"Thank you, God, for sending your son, Jesus, into the world as a little baby. Amen."**

### SHARING
Ask the children, "When you were a baby, where did you sleep?" (A crib; bassinet; cradle.) Then ask, "Does anyone know where Baby Jesus slept?" (In a manger.)

### LISTENING
Read Luke 2:1-7 from the Bible, then follow with these questions:

**Do you know what a manger is? (A trough or box which holds food such as hay for large animals.)**

Why was Jesus' first bed a manger? (Because there was no room for Mary and Joseph in the inn and they slept in the stable.)

Do you think that people were surprised that God's son was born in a place where animals lived? (Yes.)

Do you think that God was trying to surprise us? (Yes.)

Conclude by saying, "God sent Jesus to teach us and lead us. He chose to send Jesus into the world as a baby, not as a wealthy man or a king."

### EXPLORING
In this paper-folding activity, the children will use squares of construction paper to wrap the baby Jesus. Each child will need a piece of construction paper which has been trimmed into a nine-by-nine-inch square and a two-inch circle cut from pink or tan paper.

Begin the activity by giving the children the squares and circles as well as crayons and glue. Ask them to glue the circle onto one corner of the square. Next, orient the squares so that the circle is in the top corner. Have the children fold in the left and right corners, and then fold up the bottom corner.

Now that Baby Jesus is wrapped in his blanket, he needs a face. Invite the children to draw a face on the circle. If time allows, children may decorate Jesus' blanket.

### SNACKING
Serve a snack that looks like hay! Dry chow mein noodles, potato sticks, or grated cheese are easy and tasty.

### MORE EXPLORING
The children will stand in a wide circle to play the Room at the Inn game.

Begin by asking all to close their eyes. Announce: "I'm going to tap someone. That person will be the only innkeeper who has room for Baby Jesus" (tap someone). Now you may open your eyes."

Continue to explain the game, "Next, I'll choose someone to be Mary or Joseph." (Choose someone.) You will go around the circle asking, 'May I stay at your inn?' Everyone will say, 'No!' except the person whom I tapped when you all had your eyes closed. That person will answer, 'Yes, I have room in my inn.' "

When Mary or Joseph finds the person with room, it's time to start a new game. Again, tap someone secretly and choose someone to play Mary or Joseph, just as you did the first time. Continue to play as time permits or until all have had a chance to be either the innkeeper with room or Mary or Joseph.

**MORE SONGS** from *Sing a New Song*
Away in a Manger, 37
Come Softly, Walk Gently, 38
The Friendly Beasts, 39

# Jesus Is Baptized

*"Suddenly the heavens were opened to him and he saw the Spirit of God descending like a dove and alighting on him."* Matthew 3:16

### MESSAGE
Jesus was baptized and we are baptized, too.

### OPENING
Music and Movement: Oh, How I Love Jesus, page 53, *Sing a New Song*

Following Music and Movement, ask the children to sit in a circle.

### SHARING
Begin by asking the children if they have seen a baptism or know what a baptism is. After listening to their responses, explain the way that baptism is done at your church.

### LISTENING
Share the story of the baptism of Jesus, taken from chapter three of both Matthew and Luke:

Today I'm going to tell you a story about baptism and how it began. The word of God came to a man who lived in the wilderness. This wilderness man was dressed in rugged camel's hair clothes with a leather belt around his waist. His name was John.

John began traveling along the winding River Jordan preaching to people he met and baptizing them. John said that people must ask God to forgive them for the bad things they had done. John said he would make the people clean by baptizing them with water. He told everyone that he was preparing the way of the Lord. He wanted everyone to prepare their hearts for God's chosen one, Jesus.

The people who heard John the Baptizer believed him. News of John spread among the villages and into the city. People left their work and homes to go see John at the River Jordan. John was filled with the word of God and many people were baptized and made ready for Jesus.

One day Jesus came to the river to see John. John knew right away that Jesus was God's chosen one. Jesus asked John to baptize him in the water and John said, "You need to baptize me!" But Jesus explained to John that this was the right thing to do. John obeyed Jesus and baptized him. As Jesus came up from the water, he saw the heavens open and the spirit of God coming down in the form of a dove. The spirit touched Jesus and a voice from heaven said, "This is my Son, the Beloved, with whom I am well pleased."

## PRAYING

Before Children's Church begins, fill a bowl with water. To begin the prayer, ask the children to come forward, one at a time, and dip their hands into the water. Then ask them to bow their heads and fold their still wet hands as you pray:

**Heavenly Father, Thank you for John the Baptizer, who prepared the way for Jesus. Please forgive us for the bad things we do sometimes. We believe that in Jesus our sins are forgiven. Amen.**

## EXPLORING

Children will make a dove from a paper plate. Each child will need a paper plate and a pair of scissors. You will also need a hole punch and yarn.

Before Children's Church, fold each plate in half. With a pencil, draw lines on one side of the plate (see diagram). These will be guidelines for the children to follow when they cut.

Begin the craft by showing the group a paper plate dove that you have made. Give every child a folded plate and scissors, pointing out the pencil lines. Children may not be able to cut through both layers of paper plate at once, so encourage them to cut one layer first. Keeping the plate folded, the second layer may be cut by following the first cut.

To make a hanger for the dove, punch a hole in the tail somewhere along the fold line. Thread a length of yarn through the hole, and knot. Send the doves home with the children, reminding them that when Jesus was baptized, the Spirit of God came down like a dove.

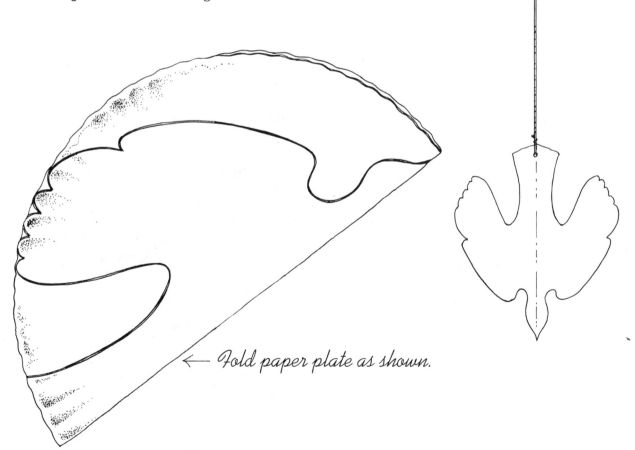

← *Fold paper plate as shown.*

## SNACKING

Bright-blue gelatin is now available. Serve this shimmering treat to represent the water of baptism.

## MORE EXPLORING

Play "Jump Over the Jordan" by rolling up the sheet from the Children's Church Kit and announcing: "This sheet is now the River Jordan where John the Baptizer baptized Jesus." As they listen to music, children are to walk in a circle "jumping over the Jordan" each time they approach the sheet. To vary the game, open the sheet to make the river wider and wider, challenging kids each time not to jump into the river and get their feet wet!

**MORE SONGS** from *Sing a New Song*

My Best Friend Is Jesus, 52
Oh, How I Love Jesus, 53
Praise the Lord, 49

---

# People Follow Jesus

*"He said to them, 'Follow me, and I will make you fish for people.' "*
*Matthew 4:19*

### MESSAGE

The fishermen followed Jesus and we follow Jesus.

### OPENING

Music and Movement: Jesus Is Calling, page 66, *Sing a New Song*

Following Music and Movement, ask the children to sit in a circle.

### LISTENING

Spread the sheet from the Children's Church Kit in the middle of the circle, then lead the group in this action story:

**Jesus was walking by the Sea of Galilee** (step in place). **He saw two brothers, Peter and Andrew** (shield eyes with hand and look from side to side). **The brothers were fishermen and they were throwing their fishing nets into the sea** (invite all to take hold of the sheet and ripple it by moving arms up and down). **Jesus said to them, 'Follow me and we can fish for people'"** (drop sheet).

**Peter and Andrew followed Jesus** (step in place). **Soon they saw fishermen in a boat** (step onto sheet and kneel or crouch). **Jesus said to them, "Follow me," and James and John left the boat** (stand up and move off the sheet, back into place in circle). **They followed Jesus** (step in place). **Jesus went throughout Galilee with his new followers: Peter, Andrew, James, and John. Jesus taught and he healed sick people. The news of Jesus spread far and wide. Soon big crowds followed Jesus wherever he went** (step in place).

### PRAYING

Have everyone around the circle hold an edge of the sheet. Ripple the sheet at the end of each line of the prayer:

**Thank you Jesus, for walking;
     we will follow you,**

**Thank you Jesus, for teaching;
     we will follow you,**

**Thank you Jesus, for healing;
     we will follow you,**

**Thank you Jesus for forgiving;
     we will follow you.**

**Amen.**

### SHARING

Say, "The disciples, Peter, Andrew, James, and John helped Jesus fish for people. They were helping people see that Jesus was God's son and that they should follow him." Ask the children, "Today, how can we help Jesus fish for people?" (Invite a friend to church; tell other people what we know about Jesus; help someone who is sick; be kind to other people.)

### EXPLORING

The children will create a fish collage using old magazines, glue, and a roll of shelf or craft paper.

Spread out the magazines and tell the children that they will "fish" for people right now by finding pictures of people in magazines. When they find a picture of a person, they are to tear out the picture of that person's face.

The length of paper you will need depends on how many pictures the children tear from the magazines. After about seven minutes, cut off an approximate length of paper and quickly pencil in a simple fish shape. Begin gluing on the faces. You may invite the children to glue on the faces, too, or they may continue to look for more pictures. To finish, write "We Fish for People" on the top of the paper and mount the fish collage on the wall.

### SNACKING

Go fishing! Gummy fish and worms or fish crackers will make for happy fishers.

### MORE EXPLORING

Catch some fun with this song and game, sung to the tune of "London Bridge."

Two children will form the "net" by facing each other, joining hands, and raising their arms and hands high, so that children can pass under their arms. The rest of the children will circle under the net. The two children forming the net will drop their arms around another child and catch him or her when everyone sings the refrain, "Jesus is our savior":

**All of us will follow him, follow him, follow him,
All of us will follow him, Jesus is our savior.**

**All of us will fish for him, fish for him, fish for him,
All of us will fish for him, Jesus is our savior.**

**All of us believe in him, believe in him, believe in him,
All of us believe in him, Jesus is our savior.**

**All of us will pray to him, pray to him, pray to him,
All of us will pray to him, Jesus is our savior.**

After singing all four verses, choose two different children to be the net, and begin again.

### MORE SONGS from *Sing a New Song*
Jesus and His Friends, 24
Jesus Loves the Little Children, 27
Jesus, Our Friend, 25

# Jesus Tells Stories

*"Everyone then who hears these words of mine and acts on them will be like a wise man who built his house on rock."*
Matthew 7:24

### MESSAGE

Jesus told stories to help people understand what he was teaching.

### OPENING

Music and Movement: The Wise Man and Foolish Man, page 68, *Sing a New Song*

Following Music and Movement, ask the children to sit in a circle.

### PRAYING

Tell children that as they listen carefully to the prayer, they should point to the body parts they hear named:

**Wonderful God,**

**I've got ears so I can hear, this story from long ago.**

**I've got a mind, so I can think, about what Jesus wants me to know.**

**I've got a mouth, so I can share, the good news of Jesus' story.**

**I've got a heart, so I can care, about living my life to his glory. Amen.**

### SHARING

This demonstration will have the children talking! You'll need two shallow bowls or baking pans and a large glass of water. In one, place the rock from the Children's Church Kit. In the other, pour a small amount of sand or salt that will serve as sand.

Begin by demonstrating what happens to both the rock and the sand when the wind blows. Invite everyone to blow first on the rock, then on the sand. Next, show what happens to the rock and sand when it rains by sprinkling water heavily on both. Continue to sprinkle water on both until they are flooded.

Ask the children, "Which can stand strong against wind, rain, and floods?" (The rock.) "On which would you build your house?" (The rock.)

### LISTENING

Make the story of the two house builders come alive with sound effects. Create sounds of rain, wind, and floods with vocal noises, or use these simple, homemade sound effects.

Rain shakers: A little unpopped popcorn in sealed paper bags.

Wind blowers: Four-by-six-inch index cards, each card rolled and taped into a tube.

Flood makers: A small amount of water in sealed plastic drink bottles.

Explain the sound effects to the children, then read Matthew 7:24-27. Emphasize the sound effect cue words: rain, floods, and winds. Children like repeating action stories, so consider reading the story a second time.

Follow the story with questions:

**In this story, Jesus told about two men who built houses. Where did the foolish man build his house? (On sand.) Where did the wise man build his house? (On rock.) What happened to the house built on sand? (It fell down.) What happened to the house built on rocks. (It did not fall down.)**

**Jesus wants us to understand that if we listen to his words and obey them we will be like the wise man who built his house on rocks, and we will also be strong like the rock.**

### EXPLORING

Let the house builders of the future have fun constructing paper houses! The building materials each child will need are six four-by-six-inch index cards, crayons, tape, and one sheet of construction paper in "rock" colors.

Give each child crayons and two cards. Tell the children that they are going to build a house. They should start by drawing the front of the house on one card and the back of the house on another. Children must orient their cards either horizontally or vertically, but not in both directions.

Next, hand out two more cards and ask the children to color the sides of their houses. When the four walls are done, you may begin to tape the sides of the card walls together. The four cards should be standing in a square. While you are doing this, the children should be given two more cards to color for the roof of the house.

When roof coloring is done, give the children a sheet of construction paper to color as a rock. Meanwhile, you can tape the roof cards together, horizontally or vertically, to suit each child's house, then tape the roof to the walls. Finally, secure the house to the rock with more tape.

### SNACKING

With saltine crackers and cheese that squirts from a canister, children can build an edible house. Peanut butter also makes a delicious mortar.

### MORE EXPLORING

Try a new twist on the old rhyme "This Is the House That Jack Built." Begin with the following version and then create your own variations with input from the children. This is also a fun rhyme to have the children act out:

This is the house that God built.

This is the child who came to the house that God built.

This is the parent who brought the child who came to the house that God built.

This is the dog that followed the parent who brought the child who came to the house that God built.

This is the neighbor who chased the dog that followed the parent who brought the child who came to the house that God built.

This is the bird that perched on the neighbor who chased the dog that followed the parent who brought the child who came to the house that God built.

This is the bug that crawled on the bird that perched on the neighbor who chased the dog that followed the parent who brought the child who came to the house that God built.

**MORE SONGS** from *Sing a New Song*
God Gifted Me, 78
I Can Make Choices, 77
If I Had a Drum, 28

*Edible Cracker House*

# Jesus Makes Miracles Happen

*"Taking the five loaves and the two fish, he looked up to heaven, and blessed and broke the loaves."*
*Mark 6:41*

### MESSAGE
Jesus made miracles happen.

### OPENING
Music and Movement: Jesus, Our Friend, page 25, *Sing a New Song,*

Following Music and Movement, ask the children to sit in a circle.

### SHARING
Rub your tummy and say, "I feel a little hungry, does anyone else feel a little hungry?" (Some will say "yes.") Continue: "When I'm really hungry, I like to eat (*fill-in*). What do you like to eat?" (Peanut butter and jelly sandwiches; cookies and milk; cereal; ice cream.)

### LISTENING
Before Children's Church, cut five loaves and two fish from construction paper. These will be used during the story. Place the loaves and fish in the basket from the Children's Church Kit. For the story, you will read the miracle of the loaves and fishes directly from the Bible, Mark 6:30-44. Pass the basket around the circle when you read verse 38.

**Introduce the story by saying, "I'm going to read to you about a time when Jesus fed a hungry crowd of five thousand people."**

**Read the story, then ask, "How do you think that Jesus was able to feed so many people from such a small amount of food?" (By his powers; it was a miracle.) Continue: "Jesus could make miracles happen through the power given to him by God."**

### PRAYING
Say this familiar children's grace as all hold hands around the circle. You may want to say the grace just before the snack, or if you don't usually serve a snack, give everyone a small treat after you say the grace:

**God is great, God is good,
Let us thank him for our food.
By his hand we all are fed,
Give us now our daily bread. Amen.**

### EXPLORING
The children will create fish place mats to use on their tables at home.

Plan to use about four pieces of construction paper per child. Some children have fewer family members, and others have more, but this should average out.

The children will decorate their place mats with crayon drawings of fish or by tracing around fish templates that you cut from index cards. To make templates, fold the card along the six-inch length and cut half of the fish shape. Unfold and flatten. Some children become frustrated when their drawing ability doesn't equal their visual ideas so templates are fun and help them get started.

Make sure the children understand what a place mat is and how it is used. Encourage them to share the story of the loaves and fishes with their families at home.

### SNACKING
Buy or bake an uncut loaf of bread and slice or break off a piece for everyone. Serve a bowl of tuna salad to use as a spread to create a delicious loaf and fish snack.

### MORE EXPLORING
Here's a fishy game to play with yarn. Each child will need a thirty-inch length of yarn. Begin by showing them how they can shape the yarn into a fish shape on the table or floor. Then, give each child a length of yarn. They can invent and reinvent their fish until the fun wears off. Next, use a

larger ball or skein of yarn to create the biggest fish ever! Everyone will cooperate to make a fish shape as large as the space will allow. When made, invite the children to walk around the yarn outline, perhaps measuring how big it is by stepping-off the distance. Children can also make their yarn lengths into smaller fish inside the giant fish.

# Jesus Heals Believers

*"Jesus turned, and seeing her he said, 'Take heart, daughter; your faith has made you well.' And instantly the woman was made well."*
*Matthew 9:22*

### MESSAGE
Jesus healed believers.

### OPENING
Music and Movement: Jesus' Hands Were Kind Hands, page 26, *Sing a New Song*
Following Music and Movement, ask the children to sit in a circle.

### SHARING
Pretend to sneeze or cough in an exaggerated way, then ask the children, "What do you do when you're sick?" (Tell my mom; go to bed; visit the doctor; say a prayer.)

### LISTENING
Tell the children today's story as a reporter for "Bible Action News." The news account is based on Matthew 9:18-31:

**My name is Jesse and I'm a kids' news reporter for the "Bible Action News." Today I saw a man, Jesus of Nazareth, rush out of my neighbor's** house. An important man from my temple was crying and leading Jesus down the street. The disciples followed and so did I. I have a nose for news!

We were hurrying down the street when a woman ran up behind Jesus and touched his cloak. Suddenly, Jesus stopped and turned around. I was surprised that he even noticed her. Jesus said, "Take heart, your faith has made you well." And right there before my eyes, she was made well. This is big news!

Well, before I could catch my breath, Jesus and the man took off down the street. When we all came around the corner, there was a crowd gathered outside the man's house. Everyone was crying and wailing and singing sad songs. Jesus shouted to the crowd, "Go away, for the girl is not dead, but sleeping." I asked an old woman if the girl was really dead. The woman said, "Yes, I saw her with my own eyes!" I waited outside the house and wondered what Jesus might do. I had seen him heal a sick woman, but could he help a dead girl?

Well, I didn't have to wait long. The man rushed out of his house laughing and shouting, "She's alive! Jesus made her live again!" Soon I saw the girl standing at the door. I was amazed. This Jesus of Nazareth must be the Son of God, because only God could have such power.

Jesus left the house. I was ready to leave too, when two blind men started following Jesus and begging loudly, "Have mercy on us!" Jesus turned to them and said, "Do you believe that I am able to do this?" When they said, "Yes, Lord," he touched their eyes and they could see again.

**I know I'm only a kid reporter, but I don't think I'll ever see a bigger, more amazing news story than this one!**

### PRAYING

Before the prayer, make a list of those in your church who are sick, and especially any children who are ill. Ask your children to hold hands around the circle and close their eyes as you pray:

**Lord of Heaven and Earth, Thank you for the people who take care of us when we are sick. We're glad that Jesus was able to heal people and show that he was truly God's son. We pray that you will help our sick friends to feel better:** (*read list*). **In Jesus' name we pray. Amen.**

### EXPLORING

Children will color the "Jesus Heals" reproducible, which is based on the Listening Story. Encourage them to decorate the cloaks and robes with colorful designs and patterns.

### SNACKING

Serve food that kids might eat when they're sick: gelatin, crackers and cola, chicken soup, or bananas.

### MORE EXPLORING

With you as the narrator, let the children act out the story from Listening. The child who plays Jesus may use the sheet from the Children's Church Kit to serve as Jesus' cloak.

### MORE SONGS from *Sing a New Song*
If I Had a Drum, 28
Jesus and His Friends, 24
Jesus, Our Friend, 25

*"Sick" Food*

Color the picture.

# Noah: Builder of the Ark

*"Make yourself an ark*
*of cypress wood."*
Genesis 6:14

### MESSAGE
God asked Noah to build the ark.

### OPENING
Music and Movement: Animal Names, page 18, *Sing a New Song*
Following Music and Movement, ask the children to sit in a circle.

### SHARING
Ask the children to say the name of their favorite animals.

### PRAYING
Have the children close their eyes and bow their heads as you pray:

**Creator God, Thank you for making so many wonderful animals. Help us to be good to animals and to share the earth with them. Amen.**

### LISTENING
As they hear the story of Noah's Ark, the children will use the palm of one hand and the fingers of the other to act out the story along with you. Begin:

**Today I'm going to tell you a well-known Bible story about animals. Can anyone guess what that story is? (Noah's Ark.) Let's use our palms and fingers to act out the story as I tell it. Place the palm of one hand flat on your lap. This is the stage. The fingers on your other hand are the actors. Watch me carefully.**

A long time ago, God was unhappy with the world. People were hurting one another (twist two fingers back and forth on palm as if they are fighting). God decided to destroy the world with a flood. He chose Noah, who was a good man, to build an ark (place one finger on palm). Noah sawed (saw two fingers back and forth) and Noah hammered (hammer with two fingers) until the ark was finished.

God told Noah to take his family (make five fingers walk across palm) into the ark. Then he told God to find two animals of each kind, male and female, to bring into the ark. Noah brought two hopping rabbits (make two fingers hop across palm) and two tiny mice (make fingers take tiny steps across palm) and two big elephants (make fingers take slow, heavy steps across palm) and two slithering snakes (slide fingers slowly across palm) and two flighty birds (make two fingers fly over palm) into the ark.

Then God made it rain (bring hand into air and down to palm several times, tapping fingers against palm) for forty days and forty nights. And the earth was flooded (place hand flat on top of palm).

After many long days, the ark came to rest on a mountain (rest fist on palm.) A little while later, Noah sent out a dove (make fingers fly off palm and about in the air) to look for a dry place to rest. But the dove couldn't find a dry place on the earth so it came back (bring fingers back to palm). A week later, Noah sent the dove out again (make dove fly from palm again). This time the dove did not return (make fingers fly behind your back). Noah knew that there was now dry land on the earth.

Noah opened the door of the ark and out came the rabbits (fingers hop) and out came the mice (fingers take tiny steps) and out came the elephants (fingers take slow, heavy steps) and out came the snakes (fingers slide across palm) and out flew the birds (fingers fly). Out came Noah's family (five fingers walk) and out came Noah (one finger walks). Then God made a rainbow appear in the sky (arch hand back and forth to form a bow) and promised to never again destroy the whole earth with a flood.

### EXPLORING

To celebrate God's promise after the flood, children will make colorful rainbows out of paper plates. Before Children's Church, cut paper plates in half and trim out the center sections.

Pass out the paper plate halves and the crayons, inviting the children to create beautiful rainbows. When the rainbows are finished, help the children punch holes in their rainbows and thread and knot a length of yarn through them. Hang the rainbows at church to create a mobile or send the rainbows home with the children.

### SNACKING

Serve animal crackers, of course! A clear soft drink or lemonade may be turned into the waters of the flood with a bit of blue food coloring.

### MORE EXPLORING

Children will have a good time playing Animal Charades. They can take turns being an animal and then call on others to guess what they are. If the children are having trouble guessing, ask questions such as "Does your animal live around here?" "Is your animal ever a pet?" or "Does your animal fly?"

**MORE SONGS** from *Sing a New Song*
Bluebird, 90
Caterpillar, 19
Go Now in Peace, 56

*Animal Crackers*

# Hannah: Turned to God in Prayer

*"There is no Rock like our God."*
1 Samuel 2:2

## MESSAGE

Hannah prayed to God.

## OPENING

Music and Movement: Little Samuel Grew, page 60, *Sing a New Song*

Following Music and Movement, ask the children to sit in a circle.

## SHARING

Have the rock from the Children's Church Kit at hand. Tell the children that you are going to send the rock around the circle. When it's their turn to hold the rock, they are each to share a story about a rock. (My dad brought me a rock from his trip to the mountains; my sister was sent to her room because she threw a rock; I collected round rocks at the lake last summer.) If the children have trouble understanding what you mean by a story about a rock, tell one or two yourself to get them started. If a child can't think of a story, he or she may just pass the rock on to the next person.

## LISTENING

Hold up the rock. Say, "I'm going to ask you some questions about this rock." Ask, "Will it break easily or is it really strong?" (It's really strong.) "Will it melt away or last a long time?" (It will last a long time.) "Does it change or does it stay about the same?" (It stays about the same.) After the questions, begin the story:

**We've been talking and thinking about rocks. I'm going to tell you a story about a woman from the Bible who thought that God was like a rock.**

**Hannah wanted a baby very much. She prayed and prayed to God. She asked God for a baby. God gave Hannah a baby boy. This baby was Samuel, who grew up to be a great prophet.**

**Hannah was happy and prayed a prayer of thanksgiving to God. Hannah's prayer is recorded in the Bible, in the book of Samuel. This is part of Hannah's prayer:**
**There is no Holy One like the Lord,**
**no one besides you;**
**there is no Rock like our God. (1 Samuel 2:2)**
**Hannah felt that God was strong and would last a long time, just like our rock. She knew that God would not change and that God would always care for her. Hannah taught her son, Samuel, to pray. Hannah had more children and she taught them to pray, too.**

## PRAYING

Say, "Since Hannah's prayer is written in the Bible, Christians can use it as a prayer today." Have the children practice saying together, "There is no rock like our God." Then, hold the rock in your hands and ask the children to stack their hands on top of it. (You may need to do the prayer in two groups if you have a lot of children.) Ask the children to close their eyes and say together, **"There is no rock like our God. Amen."**

## EXPLORING

For this activity you will need a length of shelf or craft paper. Tell the children that they are going to help you write a prayer. Hannah's prayer is a prayer of praise to God for his gift of a baby. The prayer you are going to write will be a prayer of praise, too. Consider asking your pastor if the prayer may be used in an upcoming worship service. If so, tell the children this.

Begin by writing on the paper, "Dear God, We praise you for . . ." Let each child name something for which they would like to praise God, as you write it down. When each child has added something to the prayer, write "Amen."

Ask the children to bow their heads and close their eyes as you read the prayer they have just written. If the prayer is to be used during an upcoming worship service, be sure the children are present during that part of the service. If the prayer is not to be used during worship, post it somewhere in the church for all to read, or print it in your church bulletin or newsletter.

## SNACKING

In Hannah's day, bread was often baked over a rock made hot by a fire. When cooked, the bread was flat and slightly concave, much like pita bread available in today's grocery stores. Explain this ancient baking technique to the children. Then serve them pita bread. The bread is especially good warmed and served with butter or cream cheese.

## MORE EXPLORING

Play Hannah's Stepping Stones. Cut seven rock shapes from construction paper. Arrange the rocks hopping distance apart and tape them to the floor to prevent slipping. Explain to the children that stepping stones are stones people step on to cross a stream. They are to use the stones to cross a pretend stream, saying the words, "There is no rock like our God" (one word per stone). Demonstrate; then let the children take turns.

## MORE SONGS from *Sing a New Song*

Hi-Ho, How Do I Know? 57
My Feet Stand, 62
Sing a Song of Praise, 62

# Moses: Leader of the Hebrews

*"She named him Moses, 'because,' she said, 'I drew him out of the water.' "*
*Exodus 2:10*

## MESSAGE

Moses, a baby found in the river reeds, grew up to be a leader of the Hebrews.

## OPENING

Music and Movement: Little Baby Moses, page 59, *Sing a New Song*
Following Music and Movement, ask the children to sit in a circle.

## LISTENING

Before Children's Church, wrap the doll from the Children's Church Kit in the blanket. Place the doll in the basket (if it fits) or in another basket, if practical. Hide the doll somewhere in the room. To begin the story say, "I think I hear a baby crying." Search about the room for the baby. (If your group is small, you may want to let them help you search.) When the baby has been found, bring it back to the circle and tell the story:

**Let's pretend that this is Baby Moses. One day the daughter of the king of Egypt came down to bathe in the river Nile. She saw a basket hidden among the weeds and grasses. She asked her maid to bring the basket to her. When she opened the basket, she found a baby inside. He was crying. The king's daughter felt sorry for him. She realized that he was one of the Hebrew children that her father wanted to kill. The baby's mother had hidden the baby there so the king wouldn't be able to harm him. The baby's sister watched from a distance.**

**The sister offered to find a woman to nurse the baby. The King's daughter agreed. The sister took the baby to her mother, who was, of course, also**

the baby's mother. The baby's mother took care of the baby. When he was older, she took him back to the king's daughter. The king's daughter raised him as her own son. She named him Moses, which meant "I drew him from the water."

Moses grew up to be a great prophet. A prophet is someone who gives messages to people from God. God called Moses to lead the Hebrews out of Egypt into a better place for them to live. That's how this little baby, found in a basket on the Nile River, grew up to be a very important person in the Bible.

### SHARING

Ask the children, "What would you do if you found a baby in a basket?" (Go tell a grown-up; talk to the baby; play with the baby; try to find out who the baby belonged to.)

### PRAYING

Ask the children to pretend they are holding a basket in front of them with Baby Moses inside. Then ask them to close their eyes and bow their heads and rock Baby Moses back and forth as you pray:

**God, Thank you for Moses, found in a basket, Who grew up to be a very great prophet. Amen.**

Pray the prayer again, this time asking the children to say it with you.

### EXPLORING

The children will use paper plates, crayons, paper, and a stapler to create Baby Moses in the Reeds. Make a sample to show them. Using a brown or tan crayon, color the fluted edge of the paper plate. This is the rim of the basket. Next, in the center portion of the plate, color a simple oval with a face at one end to be Baby Moses. Cut out three reeds from green construction paper, about eight-inches-high by two-inches-wide, tapered at one end. Staple the reeds onto the bottom of the paper plate to cover Baby Moses. Now Moses is hidden in the reeds. Lift the reeds to peek at Baby Moses! You will need to cut the reeds ahead of time, about three per plate. The children should be able to do the rest, with your help.

### SNACKING

Serve a snack such as pretzels or popcorn in the basket, or serveral baskets. You may want to hide the basket snack for the children to find.

### MORE EXPLORING

The children will have fun searching for Baby Moses. Ask one child to leave the room. Choose another child to hide the doll while the others watch. The first child will come back into the room and look for Baby Moses. While everyone else stays seated, the children will help the searcher by saying "hotter, hotter" when the child gets closer to the baby, and "colder, colder" as the child moves away. Let the children take turns being the searcher and the hider. In warm weather, this is a good game to play outdoors.

**MORE SONGS** from *Sing a New Song*
A Friend Is a Wonderful Thing, 84
In Our Family, 80
There's Music All Inside Me, 88

# Mary: Chosen by God

*"Do not be afraid, Mary, for you have found favor with God."*
*Luke 1:30*

### MESSAGE

God sent an angel to tell Mary that she was to be the mother of Jesus.

### OPENING

Music and Movement: An Angel Told Mary, page 35, *Sing a New Song*

Following Music and Movement, ask the children to sit in a circle.

### LISTENING

Tell the story of the angel's visit to Mary (Luke 1:26-56):

**There was a young woman named Mary who was engaged to be married to a man named Joseph. One day, before they were married, an angel visited Mary. Mary was surprised. "Do not be afraid, Mary," the angel said. "God has chosen you to give birth to his son. You will name the baby 'Jesus.'"**

**After the angel left, Mary hurried to tell her cousin Elizabeth the news. Then she said a prayer praising and thanking God for choosing her to be the mother of Jesus.**

### SHARING

Ask the children, "How would you feel if you were visited by an angel?" (Scared; surprised; I would like it.)

### PRAYING

Say, "Mary was afraid of the angel at first. But she believed that the angel was sent by God. She was happy that God had chosen her to be the mother of Jesus. Mary prayed a prayer to God that is recorded in the Bible. For our prayer today, let's pray Mary's prayer." Ask the children to close their eyes and bow their heads as you pray:

**My soul magnifies the Lord,
and my spirit rejoices in God my Savior.**
   **(Luke 1:47)**

                    **Amen.**

### EXPLORING

The children will make a colorful angel mural to decorate the church during Advent, or anytime of the year. A nursing home in your community might also appreciate a mural made by children.

From a variety of brightly colored construction paper, cut large triangles to be the angels' robes (about five inches wide at the base and about six inches high). Next, cut smaller triangles to be the angels' wings (about three inches wide at the base and three inches high). Finally, cut circles about three inches in diameter from construction paper to be the angels' faces. Cut enough shapes so that each child will be able to piece together two or three angels.

Place a length of shelf or craft paper on the table. Mix the triangles and circles together and place them in piles on the table. Show the children how to piece the shapes together to make an angel. The angels are to be glued into place. When the paper is filled with a colorful array of angels, hang the mural for all to admire or take it to a local nursing home for the patients to enjoy.

### SNACKING

Bake or purchase an angel food cake, a low fat, heavenly treat!

### MORE EXPLORING

Teach kids this action song, sung to the tune of "Here We Go Round the Mulberry Bush":

An angel visited Mary, Mary, Mary,
An angel visited Mary a long time ago (flap arms to be angel wings).

Mary was afraid, afraid, afraid,
Mary was afraid when the angel came to her (put hands over face).

The angel had good news, good news, good news,
The angel had good news, Mary would have God's son (pretend to rock baby).

Then Mary prayed, prayed, prayed,
Then Mary prayed after the angel left (kneel
and fold hands in prayer).

The children may be able to add more verses
and actions to the song, continuing on with the
Christmas Story.

# Paul: A Missionary for God

*"Paul, an apostle of Christ Jesus by the
will of God, for the sake of the promise
of life that is in Christ Jesus."*
*2 Timothy 1:1*

### MESSAGE
Paul was one of the first missionaries.

### OPENING
Music and Movement: All Around, page 73, *Sing
a New Song*
Following Music and Movement, ask the children to sit in a circle.

### SHARING
Ask the children to name a faraway place that
they have visited. Remember that to a young child,
even the next town may seem far away.

### LISTENING
Tell the children that today's story talks about a
man from the Bible who traveled to faraway places
(Acts 9:1-22):

When the Christian Church was just beginning,
after Jesus had risen into heaven, there lived a
man named Paul. Paul was a tentmaker. He
treated Christians cruelly. He had hurt many
Christians and caused some to go to prison. One
day while Paul, who was also called Saul, was traveling to the city of Damascus, a bright light from
heaven flashed around him. Jesus appeared. He
asked Paul why Paul was being cruel to Christians.
Paul became blind and couldn't see anything at
all!

Three days later, a man went to visit Paul. The
man told Paul that he was sent by Jesus to help
him regain his eyesight and to be filled with God's
love. Immediately, Paul regained his sight. Paul
believed that Jesus was the son of God. He
became a Christian and a missionary. A missionary
is someone who tells others about Jesus.

Paul traveled to lots of places, many of them far
away. Now, people sometimes treated Paul cruelly
because he was a Christian and sent him to prison.
But Paul kept his faith in God and did God's work
by telling many people about Jesus and the Christian Church. Paul wrote letters that are printed in
the Bible. Through Paul's letters, we know about
some of his travels and his work as a missionary.

### PRAYING

Make a prayer tent either before Children's Church, or with the help of the children. Stretch the sheet from the Children's Church Kit across a table or chairs. If you need to secure it, consider tying it, pinning it with safety pins, or weighting it down with heavy books. If your group is large, you may need two sheets to create a bigger tent.

When it's time for the prayer, invite the children to come inside the tent. Say, "Since Paul was a tentmaker before he became a missionary, we'll honor Paul by saying our prayer inside our own tent. Bow your heads and close your eyes while I pray":

**Dear God, Thank you for Paul, who left his job as a tentmaker and traveled to faraway places to tell other people about Jesus. We're glad that we are Christians and part of the church that Paul worked hard to begin. Amen.**

### EXPLORING

Hand each child a copy of the "Travels with Paul" reproducible and set out crayons. Explain to the children that they are to follow the dots from numbers one to twelve. Assist any children who are inexperienced with follow-the-dots. When they are finished, ask them what Christian symbol they see (a cross). If time permits, have the children color the picture.

### SNACKING

Create Paul's Trail Mix by stirring together a raisin cereal and small, chocolate candies. Serve the trail mix in small bags. You may want to have the children eat their trail mix in the tent or, weather permitting, travel outside to a pretend faraway place while snacking.

### MORE EXPLORING

For this activity you will need to talk to your pastor or denominational office about a missionary whom your church is supporting and obtain his or her address.

Explain to the children that there are missionaries today who travel to faraway places to tell others about Jesus. Tell what you have learned about a missionary whom your church is supporting. Invite the children to draw pictures to send to the missionary, since missionaries like to receive mail from home. The children may draw pictures of themselves or something or someone special to them or, weather permitting, you might take them outside to sketch the church building.

Mail the pictures to the missionary, along with a word of greeting and explanation. Hopefully, you'll receive a reply that you can share with the children!

**MORE SONGS** from *Sing a New Song*
Children Everywhere, 78
Hi-Ho, How Do I Know?, 57
We Are Messengers, 32

*Paul's Trail Mix*

# Lydia: Helper to the Church

*"The Lord opened her heart to listen eagerly to what was said by Paul."*
Acts 16:14

### MESSAGE
Lydia helped the early church.

### OPENING
Music and Movement: The Church Has Many Colors, page 34, *Sing a New Song*
Following Music and Movement, ask the children to sit in a circle.

### SHARING
Ask each child to tell his or her favorite color.

### PRAYING
Before Children's Church cut sheets of red, blue, yellow, orange, purple, and green construction paper into quarters. If your group is smaller, you can cut the paper into halves. Just before the prayer, hand a square to each child, making sure that all the colors are represented at least once. Tell the children that when they hear their color during the prayer, they are to hold their square high in the air, then bring it back down again. Practice this by calling out all of the colors. Then begin the prayer:

**Dear God, We thank you for all the world's colors. Thank you for red and blue and yellow and orange and purple and green. Thank you for lemons that are yellow and tigers that are orange and the sky that is blue and plums that are purple and cardinals that are red and lizards that are green. Amen.**

### LISTENING
Tell the story of Lydia, one of the first converts to Christianity in Europe (Acts 16:11-15):

After Jesus died and rose again on Easter Sunday, he stayed with his disciples. Then he rose into heaven. Before he left he told his disciples to tell other people about all that had happened. He wanted other people to know that he was the son of God. This is how the Christian church began. People who tell other people about Jesus are called "missionaries."

Paul was one of the first missionaries. He traveled to a place called Macedonia which was in Europe. Paul met a woman named Lydia. Lydia sold beautiful purple cloth. That's why when Christians think of purple, they sometimes think of Lydia and the beautiful purple cloth she sold.

Lydia believed what Paul told her about Jesus. She decided to become a Christian. Lydia helped Paul by inviting him to stay in her home. Some of the first church services in Europe may have been held in Lydia's home. Lydia is important because she believed in Jesus and because she helped Paul begin the church in a new place.

### EXPLORING
Children will work together to make a Color Chain. Using a variety of colors, cut nine-by-twelve-inch sheets of construction paper in three-by-twelve-inch strips. You will need a stapler to staple the chain together after the children have decorated the strips.

Introduce this activity by saying, "Just as Lydia was a helper to the early church, you are an important part of our church. I'm going to give you each a strip of colored paper. Write your name on it if you can, if not I will help you. Then decorate your strip with stripes, hearts, flowers, bugs, dots, or any design you like. When you're finished, we'll link everyone's strip together to make one beautiful, colorful chain."

Staple the strips together as the children finish them. Consider having the children present the chain to the pastor as a gift, perhaps during the worship service. You can explain to the pastor its significance. If time permits, read the names printed on the chain, since children love to hear their names read aloud.

### SNACKING

Honor Lydia by serving a purple snack such as grapes, plums, grape-flavored gelatin, or purple candy.

### MORE EXPLORING

Children enjoy playing the Color Game. Taking note of the various colors your group has on, ask everyone wearing a certain color to stand up: "If you're wearing green stand up. If you're wearing brown stand up." Play again, asking everyone wearing a certain color to stand up and twirl around. Other actions might include hopping on one foot, saying their names, clapping their hands, or shouting "Alleluia!"

### MORE SONGS from *Sing a New Song*
Children Everywhere, 78
Hi-Ho, How Do I Know?, 57
We Are Messengers, 32

*Purple Snack*

Follow the numbers and dots to travel with Paul.

6    7

4    5    8    9

3    2    11    10

1 ——————————— 12
START

## The Creation

*"God saw everything that he had made, and indeed, it was very good."*
*Genesis 1:31*

### MESSAGE
God created the world.

### OPENING
Music and Movement: God Made the Earth, page 13, *Sing a New Song*

Following Music and Movement, ask the children to sit in a circle.

### LISTENING
Children will hear the story of the creation of the world (Genesis 1–2:3). Tell them that every time you ring the bell from the Children's Church Kit they are to say together, "And it was very good." Practice once or twice, then begin the story:

**In the beginning the earth had no shape and the land was dark.**

**Then God said, "Let there be light" and there was light (ring bell).**

**And God separated the light from darkness. God called the light Day (ring bell) and the darkness Night (ring bell).**

**And there was evening and there was morning, the first day.**

**Then God made a dome over the waters. God called the dome Sky (ring bell).**

**And there was evening and there was morning, the second day.**

**Then God said, "Let the waters under the sky be gathered together in one place and let the dry land appear." God called the dry land Earth (ring bell) and he called the waters Seas (ring bell). Then God said, "Let the earth bring forth plants" (ring bell).**

**And there was evening and there was morning, the third day.**

**Then God said, "Let there be lights to make day and night and seasons and days and years." So God made the sun (ring bell) and God made the moon and stars (ring bell).**

**And there was evening and there was morning, the fourth day.**

**Then God said, "Let the waters bring forth swarms of living creatures and let the birds fly across the sky" (ring bell).**

**And there was evening and there was morning, the fifth day.**

**Then God said, "Let the earth bring forth living creatures of every kind: cattle and creeping things and wild animals of every kind" (ring bell). And God said, "Let there be humankind in God's likeness, male and female" (ring bell).**

**And God saw everything that he had made and indeed (ring bell).**

**And there was evening and there was morning, the sixth day.**

**The world was finished. On the seventh day, God rested after all that work.**

### SHARING
Hold up the rock from the Children's Church Kit. Say "This rock is part of God's creation, part of God's earth. When it's your turn to hold the rock, tell us your very favorite part of God's creation." (The ocean; clouds; caterpillars; people; the moon.)

### PRAYING
Ask the children to close their eyes and bow their heads as you pray:

**Creating God,**
**Thanks for the moon and the stars at night,**
**Thanks for the earth and the sun so bright,**
**Thanks for creatures of earth, sky, and sea,**
**Thanks for all your creation, especially me!**
**Amen.**

## EXPLORING

Teach children the old favorite, "He's Got the Whole World in His Hands." Ask them to form a circle and clap in rhythm to the song. Here are some of the traditional verses and some you can add:

He's got the whole world in his hands, he's got the whole world in his hands, he's got the whole world in his hands, he's got the whole world in his hands.

**He's got you and me, brother, . . .**
**He's got you and me, sister, . . .**
**He's got the tiny little baby . . .**
**He's got Children's Church . . .**
**He's got the town of (*your town*) . . .**

After you have sung these verses, choose two children and ask them to stand in the center of the circle. Then sing, using the names of those two children. For example, "He's got Nicky and Heather in his hands . . ." While their names are being sung, the two children can go around the circle and give everyone else "high fives" (slap right hands together). Continue sending two children at a time into the circle until everyone has had a turn.

## SNACKING

Make Edible Earths using the recipe from a box of crisped rice cereal. After the margarine and marshmallows are melted, add blue food coloring, then mix with the cereal. Grease your hands and shape the mixture into balls about two inches in diameter. The recipe should yield about twenty-five earths. Place the Edible Earths on wax paper and cover until it's time to serve them.

## MORE EXPLORING

Children can use crayons and paper plates to draw their favorite part of God's creation On two separate plates write, "Our favorite parts of God's Creation" and "Children's Church Choices." Staple these plates and the children's plates onto a length of yarn and hang them in the church for all to admire.

**MORE SONGS** from *Sing a New Song*
Who Makes the Flowers?, 15
God Plans for Many Growing Things, 16
Animal Names, 18

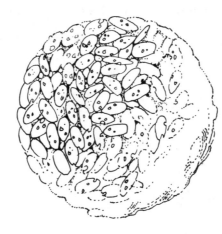

*Edible Cereal Earth*

# Plants for Food

*"I have given you every plant yielding seed that is upon the face of all the earth, and every tree with seed in its fruit; you shall have them for food."*

Genesis 1:29

### MESSAGE
God gave us plants for food.

### OPENING
Music and Movement: God Plans for Many Growing Things, page 16, *Sing a New Song*

Following Music and Movement, ask the children to sit in a circle.

### LISTENING
Tell the children that today in Children's Church they will celebrate an important and delicious part of God's creation, the fruits and vegetables that God gave us for food. Begin by asking them these riddles:

**I'm yellow and monkeys love me. (Bananas.)**

**I grow in bunches, I am small and round, and come in various colors such as green, purple, and red. (Grapes.)**

**People put me on top of their ice-cream sundaes. (Cherries.)**

**When people taste me, they pucker their lips. I make a good summertime drink. (Lemons.)**

**I'm orange and people like to drink my juice at breakfast. (Oranges.)**

**My skin is fuzzy. (Peaches.)**

**I'm fun to eat at a cookout. Kids like to see how far they can spit my seeds. (Watermelon.)**

**I'm little and green and grow in a pod. (Peas.)**

**I'm orange, I grow in the ground, and rabbits like to nibble on me. (Carrots.)**

**My stalks look like little trees. (Broccoli.)**

**I'm yellow and grow on a cob. (Corn.)**

**People make me into french fries. (Potatoes.)**

**I'm not a flower, but that's part of my name. (Cauliflower.)**

### SHARING
Ask the children to name their favorite fruit or vegetable.

### PRAYING
Ask children to kneel on the ground with their heads tucked in as if they were seeds just planted in the earth and to listen as you pray:

**Dear God, We are amazed that from a tiny seed, you can cause delicious fruits and vegetables to grow.**

Now ask the children to grow and become delicious fruits and vegetables by slowly standing up and holding their arms high in the air. Ask them to close their eyes while you pray:

**And God, Thank you for gardens of fruits and vegetables and for this garden of children! Amen.**

### EXPLORING
The children will decorate a length of craft paper with fruit shapes cut from construction paper. This table runner will add a festive touch to the serving table at your next church supper.

Before Children's Church, sketch the simple shapes of fruits and vegetables onto sheets of construction paper in the appropriate color. Some easy shapes to cut include: oranges, bananas, apples, cherries, grapes, carrots, potatoes, string beans, and peas. You will need one or two sheets per child.

Stretch a piece of shelf or craft paper the length of a table. Write "Fruits and Vegetables from God's Garden" down the middle of the paper. Explain to the children that they are going to create a table runner to decorate the serving table at your next church supper.

Hand out the construction paper and the scissors. After the children cut out the fruit and vegetable shapes, they are to glue them onto the table runner. When the table runner is dry, roll it loosely to store until a church supper. If you find it isn't practical to use the table runner at a supper, surprise the children and use it to decorate the snack table one Sunday for Children's Church.

### SNACKING
Serve a variety of sliced fruits and vegetables from God's garden.

### MORE EXPLORING
Let children take turns naming two fruits and vegetables to be used in a song. The song is sung to the tune of "Happy Birthday." For example:

**Apples and carrots from God,
Apples and carrots from God,**

**Apples and carrots taste delicious,
Apples and carrots from God.**

### MORE SONGS from *Sing a New Song*
God Made the Earth, 13
God Is So Good, 17
I'm Thankful for My Senses, 89

---

# The Seasons

*"For everything there is a season."*
*Ecclesiastes 3:1*

### MESSAGE
Seasons are part of God's plan.

### OPENING
Music and Movement: Autumn Leaves Are Now Falling, page 46, *Sing a New Song*
Following Music and Movement, ask the children to sit in a circle.

### SHARING
Remind the children that there are four seasons: spring, summer, fall, and winter. Then ask them to each tell what their favorite season is and why. (Summer because I like to go swimming; winter because I like to ice-skate; fall because my dad takes me to football games; spring because I like to look for the first robin.)

### LISTENING
Say a few words to the children about seasons:

**There is a verse in the Bible that talks about the seasons, "For everything there is a season." Seasons are part of God's plan for the earth. We can enjoy seasons. We can enjoy the changes in the weather, the changes in what grows from the earth, the changes in animal life, and the changes we make in our daily lives as we move on to each new season. Seasons make the year interesting!**

### PRAYING
Teach children this action prayer, then say it together:

**Dear God,
Thanks for spring when the earth begins to grow (crouch down, then get up slowly and spread out arms),
Thanks for winter when we watch falling snow (make fingers slowly fall to ground),
Thanks for fall when the air turns cool (cross arms across chest and shiver),
Thanks for summer when we swim in the pool (move arms and pretend to swim)!** Amen.

## EXPLORING

Announce to the children that they are now going to take a pretend walk through the seasons of the year. They should follow your lead and act out the story as you do. Make up simple actions as you tell the story and don't hesitate to be dramatic. If you live in a place where the seasons are different than those described in the prayer and the walk through the seasons, mention this to the children.

The seasons are part of God's plan. Let's take a pretend walk through the seasons. Watch me and do as I do.

It's spring. Let's bend down and see if that's a crocus popping its head up. Look over there! I think I see the first robin. Oh my! It's beginning to rain. Let's put up our umbrellas. Watch out for the mud puddle. Oh well, let's just jump in it, mud puddles are lots of fun.

Gee, it's getting hot. Maybe it's summer already. Let's take off our jackets. A pool! Let's jump in. Oh, the water is refreshing. Look! Fireworks! Cover your ears, those booms are loud. It must be the Fourth of July. Look at the corn in that vegetable garden over there. I bet that will be delicious!

My, the air seems to be getting crisp. It's fall! Let's put our jackets back on. The trees are orange and yellow, and leaves are falling down. Let's rake a pile and jump in it. I see a pumpkin on the neighbor's porch. (Sniff.) Is that turkey I smell? Why it must be Thanksgiving already.

I don't believe it. Snow! Let's throw some snow-balls. Happy winter! Look how bare those trees are. Some trees are still green. Those are ever-greens. They stay green all year long; that's why we use them for Christmas trees. Do I hear carolers singing Christmas carols? Let's go ice-skating. Gosh, this is a cold winter.

I think I feel a little warmer. Yes, it's warming up. The snow has melted. Do I see a robin over there? It's spring. We've taken a walk through all the seasons of the year.

## SNACKING

In honor of two of the seasons, summer and winter, serve a silly snack: frozen fruit pops and hot chocolate!

## MORE EXPLORING

Choose Christian music that represents the four seasons to sing with the children: Palm Sunday and Easter songs for spring, songs about nature and the earth for summer, Thanksgiving songs for fall, and Christmas songs for winter.

**MORE SONGS** from *Sing a New Song*
March, 87
Bluebird, 90
Praise the Lord, 49

# Creatures! Creatures!

*"So God created the great sea monsters and every living creature that moves."*
Genesis 1:21

### MESSAGE
God made wonderful creatures.

### OPENING
Music and Movement: Animal Names, page 18, *Sing a New Song*

Following Music and Movement, ask the children to sit in a circle.

### SHARING
Hold up the toy animal from the Children's Church Kit and ask, "What type of creature is this?" (A bear, a dog.) Explain to the children that this week you are talking about the creatures that God created. You will pass the toy animal around the circle. They are to give it a hug, saying, "I like (*type of toy animal*) and I like (*their favorite animal*)."

### LISTENING
(If you can locate a book with photographs or illustrations of sea creatures, bring it along to show to the children.) Begin:

**Listen to this Bible verse: "So God created the great sea monsters and every living creature that moves." Just imagine! There are creatures all over the earth that we probably won't ever see, but it's fun to know that they exist and to learn a little bit about them. The Bible verse talks about great sea monsters. Let me tell you about three of them:**
**There are giant squids with ten arms. On the arms are rows of suction cups. The squid uses the suction cups to grasp onto creatures they want to capture and eat. The giant squid can grow to be as long as ten people.**
**The blue whale is probably the biggest creature in the world. The whale eats krill, which are tiny animals about two-inches long, that look like shrimp. The blue whale can eat as much as four tons of krill in one day.**

**The octopus has eight arms with suction cups, called tentacles, that it uses to wrap around its prey. If another animal is chasing it, the octopus can let out a dark-black liquid that makes a cloud that hides the octopus while it escapes.**
**These are just three of the thousands of amazing creatures that God put in the oceans.**

### PRAYING
Ask the children to close their eyes and bow their heads.

Say, "I'm going to count from one to five. Each time I say a new number, picture in your minds a different creature that God created. Ready?"

**One . . . two . . . three . . . four . . . five. . . . Thank you God, for the wonderful and amazing creatures of your world. Amen.**

### EXPLORING
Create a colorful undersea mural using crayons and a length of shelf or craft paper. While not necessary, a blue wash can be applied over the mural when the coloring is finished. Simply mix ten to fifteen drops of blue food coloring to ½-cup water. The children will enjoy applying the wash with brushes, or you can do this at a later time.

Tell the children that since there are so many wonderful creatures in the ocean, they may use their imaginations to create any type of sea creature they like. Encourage them to color heavily and use vibrant colors. When the mural is finished, ask all to step back and admire it. Apply the blue wash if you've chosen to do so. Label the mural "God's Wonderful Sea Creatures" and hang it for all to see.

### SNACKING
Cut squares of cheese slices into triangles (four per slice). Hand each child four oval crackers, four cheese triangles, and four or more raisins. Explain that many fish travel in groups called "schools." They are to arrange the shapes you've given them into a school of four fish. After the schools have been created, they may be consumed!

## MORE EXPLORING

Bring out the modeling dough and let the children go to work creating any creature they like. If time permits, they can each introduce their creature, perhaps giving it a silly name.

## MORE SONGS from *Sing a New Song*

Caterpillar, 19
Bluebird, 90
God Plans for Many Growing Things, 16

---

# Caring for God's Earth

*"The land shall not be sold in perpetuity, for the land is mine."*
*Leviticus 25:23*

### MESSAGE

God wants us to take care of the earth.

### OPENING

Music and Movement: God Made the Earth, page 13, *Sing a New Song*

Following Music and Movement, ask the children to sit in a circle.

### LISTENING

As children listen to the following situations, they are to respond by giving a "thumbs up" or a "thumbs down." You may want to offer a word of explanation after each situation. Begin by saying:

**God has given us the earth to live on and enjoy, but God expects us to take good care of the earth. Listen to the following situations and give me "thumbs up" if the child is taking good care of the earth, and "thumbs down" if the child is hurting the earth.**

**Gray helped his grandfather plant trees. (Thumbs up.)**

**Robin threw her soda can into the trash basket instead of the recycling bin. (Thumbs down.)**

**Sarah tossed her candy wrappers out the car window. (Thumbs down.)**

**Jonathan and Chris picked up litter they found in the woods. (Thumbs up.)**

**Gwen threw her plastic sandwich bag into the stream. (Thumbs down.)**

**After the ice storm, Kevin put out food for the birds and squirrels. (Thumbs up.)**

**Caroline and Heidi helped their mother take their old clothes and toys to the thrift shop instead of throwing them away. (Thumbs up.)**

**Juan forgot to turn off the hose and left it running all afternoon. (Thumbs down.)**

**Kisha was careful to turn off her light when she left her room. (Thumbs up.)**

### SHARING

Ask the children to tell ways that they can help take care of the earth. (Don't litter; recycle; don't waste water and electricity; plant trees.)

### PRAYING

Have the children stand and make their arms form a circle to represent the earth. Ask them to close their eyes as you pray:

**Dear God, Thank you for making the earth and giving it to us. We promise to do our best to take care of the earth and everything in it. Amen.**

### EXPLORING

The children will turn luncheon size paper bags into litter bags to be kept in the family car or another convenient place.

Before Children's Church, make copies of the "Friends of the Earth" reproducible. The reproducible will be cut in half so you will need one copy for every two children. After the reproducibles are made, cut each one in half horizontally. Children will color the two designs, cut them out, and glue them on each side of the paper bag.

Before you hand out the supplies, remind the children that one of the best ways that kids can help take care of the earth is by making sure they put their trash in a trash container, not on the ground. Tell them that they are going to make litter bags, which are just perfect to keep in the car to hold small bits of trash. If some of the families in your church do not use a car, tell children that the litter bags may be kept in some other convenient place.

Give each child a bag and the reproducible designs. Set out scissors, crayons, and glue. Ask the children to color the designs, cut them out, and glue them to both sides of the bag.

### SNACKING

Many children don't eat their bread crusts, much to the dismay of their parents! Show children something they can do with their bread crusts, if they don't want to eat them. Prepare peanut butter and jelly sandwiches and cut the crusts off ahead of time. Put the crusts in a bag. As the children eat their sandwiches, bring out the crusts. Tie the crusts along a length of yarn, saying, "I know that some kids don't like bread crusts, but look what we can do with them. Instead of throwing them away, we can hang them on a tree to feed the birds."

Weather permitting, take the children outside to the churchyard. Let them help you select a tree that is not too close to the building on which to hang the crusts.

### MORE EXPLORING

Ask the children to sit or stand in a circle. Hold up the ball from the Children's Church Kit and say, "Let's pretend that this ball is the earth." Explain that when the ball is rolled to them they are to pick it up, hug it, and say, "I'll do my best to take care of God's earth," then roll the ball to someone else.

**MORE SONGS** from *Sing a New Song*
God Is So Good, 17
Jesus Saw the Flowers, 24
Jesus Loves the Little Children, 27

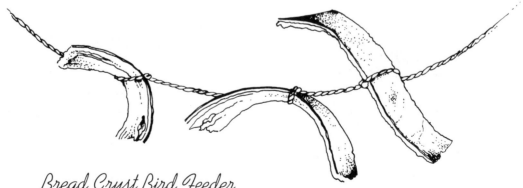

*Bread Crust Bird Feeder*

# Close to God

*"I lift up my eyes to the hills—from where will my help come? My help comes from the LORD, who made heaven and earth."*
*Psalm 121:1-2*

### MESSAGE
Nature makes us feel close to God.

### OPENING
Music and Movement: Who Makes the Flowers? page 15, *Sing a New Song*

Following Music and Movement, ask the children to sit in a circle.

### LISTENING
Begin by reading the Bible verses (Psalm 121:1-2). Then say:

**These verses are from the book of Psalms. A psalm is a poem or song written to God. The person who wrote this song might have been outside and looked up at the hills of the Holy Land. God doesn't live in the hills. God is everywhere, but by looking at the beauty of the world God created, we can feel closer to God. The person who wrote this psalm may have looked up at the beautiful hills and felt closer to God.**

### SHARING
Explain to the children the difference between what is natural and what is man-made. Ask them to each tell about a favorite natural place they have visited. (We go to my grandma's cabin in the mountains; we went on a hike and ate lunch by a waterfall; I like to sit by a stream in my backyard; I think the beach is really beautiful.)

### PRAYING
Ask the children to bow their heads and close their eyes as you pray:

**Dear God who created the world, Help us to look at your beautiful places: the lakes and streams, the mountains and fields, the oceans and deserts, and feel close to you. Amen.**

### EXPLORING
In warm weather, consider taking the children outside to a peaceful spot for this activity. Inside or outside, ask the children to spread out and make themselves comfortable. They may even lie down if this is practical. Begin by saying:

"We are going to take a pretend vacation to see some of the natural wonders that God created. The vacation will take place in your imaginations. Close your eyes, relax, and let your minds go to work as you listen to me.

(Speak slowly and calmly.) We've left the church and we're on our way. The first place we are visiting is a gently rolling stream in the woods. We can hear the stream gurgle over the rocks. God, we feel your presence as we rest by this stream.

Now we are high in the mountains. The view is magnificent. We can smell pine trees and we can hear the wind whistling. God, we feel close to you as we stand on the top of these mountains.

Now we are rowing a boat in a lake. The water is calm and blue. We can see fish swimming below the surface and a mother duck leading her ducklings into the lake. God, we praise you for this lake and the creatures of your world.

The next place we're visiting is a meadow. The meadow is flat and we can see for miles. There are blue and yellow wildflowers and the sky is filled with puffs of white clouds. As we look about, God, we know that you are with us.

Now we're in a desert. Lizards are darting from under the rocks. We're sitting next to a cactus that is taller than we are. Look! There's a roadrunner. Thank you, God, for this desert.

Our last stop is at the beach. Our feet dig into the cool sand as we walk. The surf comes up and splashes us. We can taste the salt air as the wind whips past us. But listen, I hear the church bell calling! It's time to go back. God, thank you for this beach and for all the natural places in your world. Amen.

### SNACKING
Children won't be able to resist Munchy Mountains. Purchase canned whipped cream and graham crackers. Help the children squirt dollops of whipped cream onto the graham crackers. They have just created snow covered mountains that are beautiful and delicious!

## MORE EXPLORING

Children will make Star Circles to wear around their necks as prayer reminders. Cut circles two inches in diameter from black or dark blue construction paper. Cut lengths of yarn about thirty-six-inches in length. Have foil stars and a hole punch at hand.

Tell children that their imaginary trip took place in the daytime but that being outdoors at nighttime, too, can help them feel close to God. Some people like to look up to the stars at night, think about God, and say a prayer. Tonight they are to look up at the stars and say a prayer. To help them remember, they'll make star circles to wear around their necks.

Pass out the circles and the foil stars, telling the children to turn the circles into a starry sky. Help the children punch holes in the circles, thread them with a length of yarn, and knot the yarn. Ask the children to wear their star circles as reminders to go outside that night, look at the stars, and say a prayer. Afterward they can hang their star circles in their rooms. Tell them that if the stars aren't out due to cloudy skies, they can still say a prayer as they look up at the sky.

**More Songs** from *Sing a New Song*
Happy All the Time, 94
Thank You, God, for Loving Me, 81
Thankful Am I, 79

*Prayer Reminder*

Cut on dotted lines. Color and cut out circles. To make a litter bag, glue circles to paper bag. *Hooray for Children's Church* Copyright © 1995 Abingdon Press.

*"Let your light shine before others, so that they may see your good works and give glory to your Father in heaven."*
*Matthew 5:16*

### MESSAGE
Christians show love for all to see.

### OPENING
Music and Movement: This Little Light of Mine, page 67, *Sing a New Song*
Following Music and Movement, ask the children to sit in a circle.

### SHARING
Have the children share their feelings about darkness. (It scares me; I can't find my way around; I leave a light on at night.)

### LISTENING
The following story is written to help children understand what it means for Christians to let their lights shine. Have a Bible marked to Matthew 5:14-16:

**Most of us are afraid of the dark at some time or another. We can't see in darkness and that's why lights are nice. There's a verse in the Bible that tells us that as Christians we are the light of the world. We shouldn't hide our light, but let it shine. Listen to a story that helps explain what this means.**

**Holly liked to visit the elderly woman, Mrs. Mulligan, who lived next door to her. Mrs. Mulligan couldn't walk very well and she lived all by herself. Holly often helped Mrs. Mulligan. She carried in her newspaper, dusted her coffee table, swept her** porch, and kept her company. She brought Mrs. Mulligan pictures that she painted in school, flowers from the garden, and chocolate chip cookies that she and her mother had baked. Sometimes, Holly and Mrs. Mulligan said prayers together, thanking God for flowers or friends or chocolate chip cookies.

**One cloudy, winter day, it was a little too dark in Mrs. Mulligan's house. Holly jumped up and turned on the light by Mrs. Mulligan's chair.**

**"You remind me of a verse in the Bible, Holly,"** Mrs. Mulligan said. **"Bring me my Bible from the table and I'll read it to you."**

**Holly brought Mrs. Mulligan her Bible and listened while she read.** (Open your Bible and read Matthew 5:14-16.)

**Mrs. Mulligan closed her Bible and looked at Holly. Then she said, "Because you are good to me and help me, you are showing me Christian love. You are like a light that brightens my loneliness. Thank you, Holly."**

### PRAYING
Ask the children to put their thumbs under their chins with their palms facing out and their fingers spread apart. Tell them to put big smiles on their faces, for now they look just like lights. Ask them to close their eyes while you pray:

**Dear God, Make us lights of the world. As we show Christian love and help others, let our lights shine for all to see. Amen.**

### EXPLORING
With this situation game, children will turn themselves into lights, as they did for the prayer, when you describe someone acting as a light. They will cover their eyes when you describe someone acting as darkness. Explain this and begin:
Randall kicked Jamal. (Darkness.)
Stephanie gave Cliff half of her ice-cream sandwich. (Light.)

At Children's Church, Quang and Kevin refused to speak to the new boy. (Darkness.)

Maria invited her cousin to church. (Light.)

Katherine and Kirsten pinched each other. (Darkness.)

Hannah threw a toy truck at Roberto. (Darkness.)

Eric sent his grandfather a birthday card. (Light.)

Zack brought cookies for Pastor Witt. (Light.)

When Mr. Tatter said "hello" outside the church, Tim ignored him. (Darkness.)

Shirmika helped entertain the babies in the nursery. (Light.)

Emily and her father took tomatoes they had grown to all their neighbors. (Light.)

Maggie threw a rock at her grandma's cat. (Darkness.)

Carlos watched his baby cousin while his aunt fixed dinner. (Light.)

### SNACKING

Explain that we often light candles in church to remind us that God sent Jesus to light up the world, and that Christians make the world brighter by their good works. Serve the snack by candlelight, making sure the children don't touch the candles. Consider serving chocolate chip cookies since they are mentioned in the story.

### MORE EXPLORING

Make candles from sheets of yellow construction paper. Cut a sheet of nine-by-twelve-inch paper in half lengthwise and then cut each half into six strips about two inches wide. Before the activity, hide the candles in simple hiding places.

Invite the children to search for the candles, explaining that each child is to find just one. After the candles are found, help the children write their names down the length of the candles. Punch a hole in the candles, tie a thirty-six-inch length of string through each one, and knot. Ask the children to wear their lights for all to see!

**MORE SONGS** from *Sing a New Song*
My Feet Stand, 62
Hi-Ho, How Do I Know?, 57
We Are Messengers, 32

# Good Samaritans

*"But a Samaritan while traveling come near him; and when he saw him, he was moved with pity."*
Luke 10:33

### MESSAGE
Christians care for people who are sick or hurt.

### OPENING
Music and Movement: Jesus' Hands Were Kind Hands, page 26, *Sing a New Song*
Following Music and Movement, ask the children to sit in a circle.

### SHARING
Ask the children to each talk about times when they were sick or hurt. Who took care of them? (My mom took me to the hospital when I broke my arm; my grandma kept me when I had the flu; my dad pulled out a big splinter.)

### LISTENING
The story of the Good Samaritan may be read directly from the Bible (Luke 10:30-37). Explain that in Bible times Samaritans and Jews were not friends. The man who was hurt was Jewish. Read the story. After the reading, ask the children questions to make certain they understood the story:

**What happened to the man who was traveling from Jerusalem to Jericho? (He was beaten by robbers.)**

**Did the priest stop and help him? (No.)**

**Did the next man, a Levite, stop and help him? (No.)**

**Did the Samaritan stop and help him? (Yes.)**

**What did the Samaritan do to help him? (He bandaged his wounds, let him ride on his animal, took him to an inn and cared for him, paid his bill at the inn.)**

**Which of these three men treated the hurt man the right way? (The Samaritan.)**

**Conclude by saying, "Jesus told this story. He wants Christians to care for people who are sick or hurt."**

### PRAYING
Tell the children to form a circle, then turn sideways to put their hands on the shoulders of the person in front of them. Ask them to close their eyes as you pray:

**Loving God, Help all of us to be like the Good Samaritan and take care of people when they are sick or hurt. Amen.**

### EXPLORING
Children will make get well cards by gluing pictures they cut from magazines onto construction paper. If you think your children will have trouble selecting and cutting out pictures, you can do this ahead of time.

Explain to the children that one of the ways that Christians can help those who are sick or hurt is by sending them get well cards. Get well cards remind people that we care for them and that we are thinking about them and praying for them. Get well cards cheer people up!

Show the children how to fold the construction paper in half. Encourage them to look through the magazines for silly or pretty pictures that might cheer someone up who is sick or hurt (if you haven't cut out the pictures for them). Then, ask them to glue the pictures to the front of the card. Those who know how to write may want to write a simple message such as "Get Well Soon" and sign their names. You can help those who don't yet write sign their names, and you can add messages later if that's more convenient.

The cards can be delivered, by mail or in person, to members of your congregation who are sick or injured. If you are fortunate enough to have a healthy congregation at the moment, give the cards to your pastor to deliver when he or she sees a need.

### SNACKING
Serve the most traditional of get well foods, chicken noodle soup. Make sure the soup is not too hot. Oyster crackers or saltines are favorites with soup.

**MORE EXPLORING**

Use the stuffed animal and the sheet to help children act out a more contemporary version of the Good Samaritan. Choose the injured person and have him or her lie down on the floor. Have a whole line of children walk up to the person, shake their heads or pretend not to see, and walk away. The last person in line can stop to help by covering up the injured person and tucking him or her in with the stuffed animal.

**MORE SONGS** from *Sing a New Song*

Jesus, Our Friend, 25
If I Had a Drum, 28
We Are Messengers, 32

114

# Cheerful Givers

*"God loves a cheerful giver."*
*2 Corinthians 9:7*

## MESSAGE
God wants us to be happy when we give.

## OPENING
Music and Movement: Love One Another, page 82, *Sing a New Song*

Following Music and Movement, ask the children to sit in a circle.

## LISTENING
For the following story, ask the children to supply some information that you will fill into the blanks as you tell the story. Explain that they are going to help you write the story. Ask them to name: a month of the year; a day of the week; a color; a type of animal; a boy's name; a girl's name; and a silly name. Jot down their answers, then begin the story:

**God wants us to be cheerful givers. The story I am going to tell you is about a cheerful giver named (boy's name).**

**One (day of week) in (month), (boy's name) went into his kitchen.**

**His mother said, "I just heard that (girl's name) has had an accident. She hurt her leg and has to rest on the couch until it's better. She's upset because she's going to miss her best friend's birthday party and also her trip to the zoo with her class."**

**"That's awful," said (boy's name). "I wish I could think of something to make her feel better."**

**Suddenly he had an idea! "I know," he said. "I'll give her my (color) toy (animal) that I got for my birthday."**

**(Boy's name) and his mother went to see (girl's name). She loved the (color) (animal) and she kept it with her on the couch. She named it (silly name) and treasured it always. And (boy's name) felt happy because he had made his friend (girl's name) happy.**

**Now that's the story of a cheerful giver.**

## SHARING
Ask the children to each tell of a time when they gave happily. (I brought old toys to the thrift shop; I put a quarter in the offering plate; I brought Nathan a birthday present; I gave my grandma a bunch of flowers I picked.)

## PRAYING
Teach children this prayer, sung to the tune of "Kum Ba Ya," then sing it together:

**Make us cheerful givers, Lord we pray,**
**Make us cheerful givers, Lord we pray,**
**Make us cheerful givers, Lord we pray,**
**Oh Lord, this we pray.**

## EXPLORING
Children will turn paper luncheon size bags into gift bags. Plan on three to four bags per child. Fold over and crease the top two inches of each bag. Next, cut circles three inches in diameter out of construction paper (three per bag). The children will also need crayons and glue.

Explain to the children that they are going to make Cheerful Giver Gift Bags. Tell them that the bags are perfect for holding a small present or homemade treat for someone special. Children can turn the construction paper circles into happy faces and glue them onto the bags.

When parents arrive to pick up their children, say a word about the gift bags. After a gift is placed inside, the bags can be secured with ribbon threaded through punched holes, a sticker, staples, or tape.

### SNACKING

The children can celebrate cheerful giving by squirting cheese from a canister onto round crackers to create happy faces.

### MORE EXPLORING

Divide the children into pairs and let them use the modeling dough to make pretend gifts for one another. If time permits, let them change partners and make more gifts.

**MORE SONGS** from *Sing a New Song*

We're Going to Our Church, 30
The Things We Need, 92
The Family of God, 80

*Happy Snack*

# Pennies for the Church

*"Truly I tell you, this poor widow has put in more than all of them."*
*Luke 21:3*

### MESSAGE
We give money to the church.

### OPENING
Music and Movement: Thankful Am I, page 79, *Sing a New Song*

Following Music and Movement, ask the children to sit in a circle.

### SHARING
Show the children two pennies and ask, "What's this?" (Money; pennies.) Next, ask the children to tell some of the things that their family buys with money. (Groceries; toys; cheeseburgers; movie tickets; sneakers.)

### LISTENING
Introduce the subject of giving money to the church and then tell the story of the Widow's Mite from Luke 21:1-4.

**Families need money to buy lots of things. Churches need money, too. Churches need money to pay the minister, to pay the water and heating bills, to buy supplies for the Sunday school, the office, and the choir, and to buy lots of other things that they need. Churches also give money away to people and organizations who need help. When we collect our offering in Sunday school and in church, we are collecting money for our church to use.**

**The Bible tells us that God doesn't care how much money we give to the church. God only cares that we give as best we can. Once, Jesus was in the temple. He saw rich people giving lots of money. Then he saw a poor woman who only gave (hold up the pennies) two coins. Jesus said, "Truly I tell you, this poor [woman] has put in more than all of**

them." Jesus knew that the woman had given all that she could.

### PRAYING
For the prayer activity and other activities this week, children will be given pennies to hold. Warn children not to put the pennies in their mouths. They might choke. Do not give pennies to children under four years of age.

Have the basket from the Children's Church Kit and the container of pennies at hand. Pass out two pennies to each child. Say "We are going to think about the poor woman as we each put two coins into the basket." Invite the children to come forward, one at a time, and place their pennies in the basket. When all the pennies have been collected, ask the children to bow their heads and close their eyes as you pray:

**Dear God, Help us to remember the poor woman in the temple. Even though she was poor, she gave all she could. Help us to share our money with our church. Amen.**

### EXPLORING
The children will make penny rubbings using white paper, pennies, and crayons. Give each child a sheet of paper and two pennies. Set out the crayons. Show the children how to fold their paper in half and place the pennies inside. Then demonstrate how to rub the crayon over the paper until the pattern of the pennies appears. Pennies tend to slip about so it's helpful to hold thumb and forefinger on the top sheet over the pennies to secure them. The pennies can be moved to new locations inside the folded sheet and more rubbings made until everyone has a page of pennies.

### SNACKING
Make coins by wrapping vanilla wafers or other round sturdy cookies with aluminum foil. Serve the cookies in a round bowl or basket. Encourage the children to use their imaginations and pretend that they are looking at coins in the offering plate! Of course, unlike those collected in church, these coins can be unwrapped and eaten.

**MORE EXPLORING**

Have the children form a circle for a penny toss. Place the basket from the Children's Church Kit in the center of the circle. Give each child two pennies. Invite the children to try and toss the pennies into the basket saying "Even a little helps a lot" as they toss. They can pick up any pennies that don't make it into the basket after everyone has had a chance to toss.

**MORE SONGS** from *Sing a New Song*
Love One Another, 82
We're Going to Our Church, 30
The Family of God, 80

*"Even a little helps a lot."*

# Working at Church

*"I will know that you are standing firm in one spirit, striving side by side with one mind for the faith of the gospel."*
Philippians 1:27

### MESSAGE
Christians work together for their church.

### OPENING
Music and Movement: We're Going to Our Church, page 30, *Sing a New Song*

Following Music and Movement, ask the children to sit in a circle.

### SHARING
Ask the children to each tell one way that they help at home. (Clean up my toys; clear the table; sweep the porch.)

### LISTENING
Introduce this action story, then ask the children to listen carefully and act it out. If they are reluctant to act without your lead, do the actions yourself.

**Just as we help at home, Christians work together and help at church, too. As I read the story, I want you to listen carefully and act out the ways that people are helping at church.**

**Some of us help by singing in the choir (pretend to hold a book and sing).**

**Some of us help by welcoming visitors (shake hands with those around you).**

**Some of us help by washing dishes (pretend to scrub dishes).**

**Some of us help by rocking babies (pretend to rock baby in arms).**

**Some of us help by painting walls (pretend to dip brush in bucket and paint).**

**Some of us help by raking leaves (pretend to rake leaves).**

**Some of us help by cooking dinners (pretend to stir and then taste food).**

**Some of us help by counting the money (pretend to count money).**

**Some of us help with our smiling faces (smile). There are lots of ways to help at church!**

### PRAYER
Have the children stand close together in a circle. Say, "Listen to this Bible verse that talks about Christians helping at church." Read Philippians 1:27 (above). Next, ask them to stay close together with sides touching, and to close their eyes and bow their heads as you pray:

**Dear God, We're glad that we can work together, side by side, to help our church. Amen.**

### EXPLORING
Teach children this song that uses the ideas and actions from the story. It's easy to change the wording to fit the song, as is shown in the first verse below. The song is sung to the tune of "Here We Go Round the Mulberry Bush."

This is the way we sing in the choir (pretend to hold book), sing in the choir, sing in the choir,

This is the way we sing in the choir, we're working together at church.

Refer to the Listening story and sing the rest of the song in this fashion, using actions with each verse.

### SNACKING
Have the children work together to prepare the day's snack. Consider a snack such as peanut butter and crackers, and juice. Some children can set out napkins and cups, some can spread peanut butter on the crackers, some can pour the juice, and some can serve the snack. Those that didn't get to help prepare the snack can help with cleanup.

## MORE EXPLORING

The children can work together to make something for the church such as bulletin covers or paper banners. The authors' book, *Creative Ways to Offer Praise: One Hundred Ideas for Sunday Worship* (Abingdon Press), suggests many simple yet eye-catching decorations that children can make for the worship service. (See the life-size paper angel below.) On the Sunday that the decorations are used, make certain that the children see their artwork and understand their contribution to the worship service.

**MORE SONGS** from *Sing a New Song*
Thankful Am I, 79
The Things We Need, 92
Come! Come! Everybody Worship!, 31

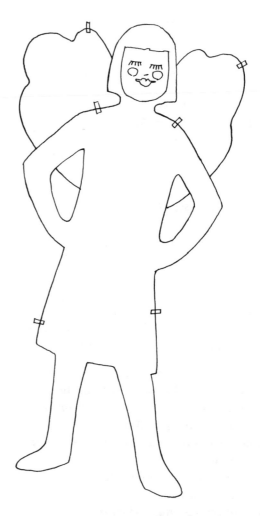

# Proclaiming the Good News

*"And they went out and proclaimed the good news everywhere."*
*Mark 16:20*

### MESSAGE
We invite people to our church.

### OPENING
Music and Movement: We Are Messengers, page 32, *Sing a New Song*

Following Music and Movement, ask the children to sit in a circle.

### LISTENING
Children will hear that Christians are to tell others about Jesus. Then they will help write a newspaper about their church. Have a length of shelf or craft paper at hand, and a crayon for writing. Begin by saying:

**In Bible times, after Jesus had risen into heaven, his disciples went and told others the good news that Jesus was God's son. This is how the Christian Church began. Today, we want people to come to our church to hear the good news about Jesus.**

**One way that people learn news is by reading the newspaper. Let's write a newspaper that tells other people about our church. First, I'll write *The (your church's name) Newspaper* at the top. (Do this.) Now, what do we want to tell other people about our church?**

Let the children tell you about the church and then write it on the paper. You may need to prompt them or reword what they say. The newspaper might read something like this:

We worship God at our church.
Our church is made of red bricks.
We have fun in Sunday school and Children's Church.
Last week we had a potluck supper.
Our steeple fell down in a big storm.
Our pastor is nice.
We sing hymns and say prayers.
We learn about Jesus.
For the final line, write, "Please come to our church."

When the newspaper is finished, read it back to the children. After Children's Church, hang the newspaper for all to see, perhaps in a location where others who use your church building but don't attend your church will see it.

### SHARING
Ask the children to each give the name of someone they could invite to church.

### PRAYING
Ask the children to close their eyes and bow their heads as you pray:

**Dear God, We come to church to hear the good news about your son, Jesus. Help us to remember to invite people to our church and to make them feel welcome when they visit. Amen.**

### EXPLORING
Children will decorate the "Good News Invitation" reproducible. Plan on one copy of the reproducible per child.

Hand out the invitations and set out the crayons. Explain that these are invitations to your church. Ask the children to think about someone they would like to invite to church, as they color the invitations. They should use a different color crayon to fill in each section of the stained-glass cross. After they are home, their parents can help them fill in the invitation and give them to the person their child would like to invite.

Say a word to parents about the invitations when they arrive to pick up their children.

### SNACKING
Cover the snack table with a tablecloth of newspaper. Children will especially appreciate dining on the comics and sports sections.

## MORE EXPLORING

Let the children take part in the Good News Whisper Line. Line the children up a few feet apart. Whisper a phrase into the first child's ear. That child will then whisper the phrase to the next child. This continues down the line until the last child says the phrase aloud for all to hear. Comparing the original phrase to the phrase the last child heard often results in lots of laughter. Some phrases for the Whisper Line might be: "Jesus is God's Son," "Hear the good news about Jesus," or "Please come to church with me."

## MORE SONGS from *Sing a New Song*

Reproducible for Section 9:  Sharing  and Giving — Program:  Proclaiming the Good News — Title:  "Good News Invitation"

*Hooray for Children's Church*   Copyright © 1995 Abingdon Press.

Color the stained-glass window and fill in the blanks.

# THE GOOD NEWS

*SPECIAL EDITION*

**BIBLE TIMES**

*SPECIAL EDITION*

Dear _____,

Please come
to church
with me

on _____

Love, _____

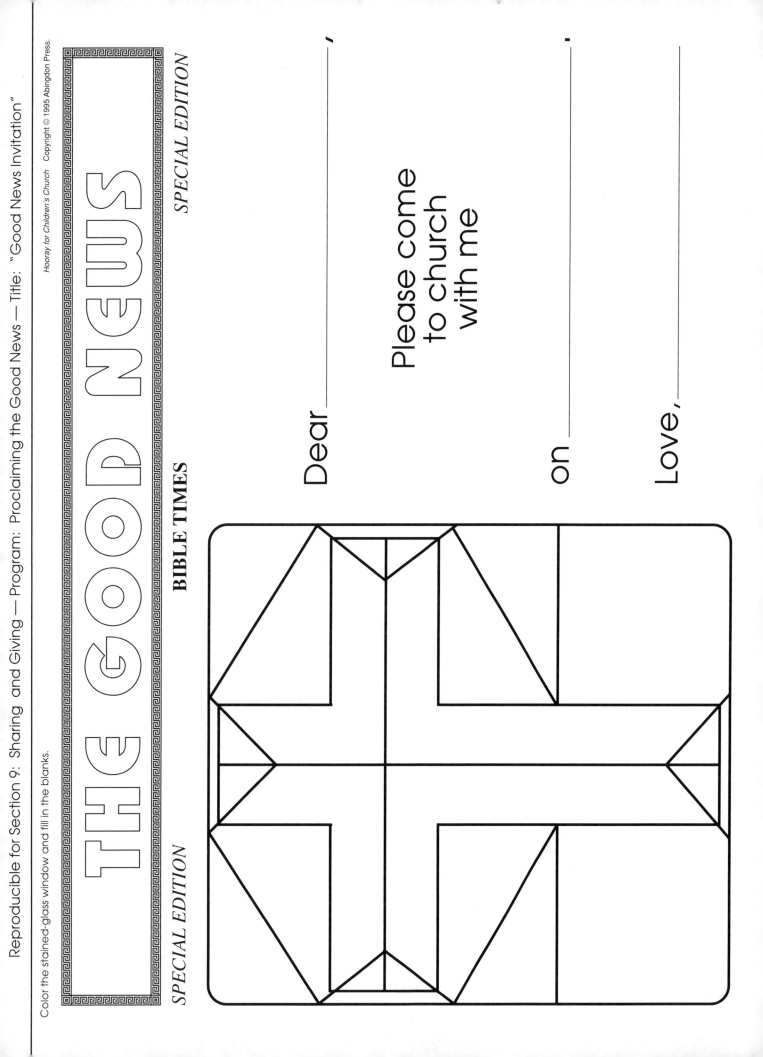

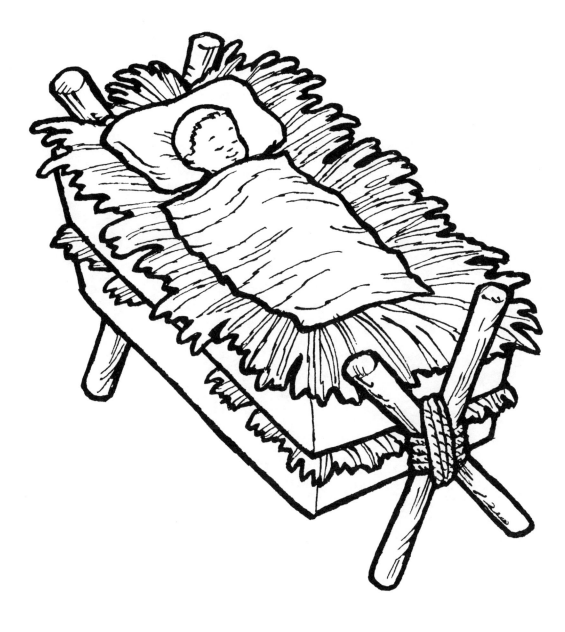